BEYOND ANTHROPOLOGY

BEYOND ANTHROPOLOGY

SOCIETY AND THE OTHER

BERNARD McGRANE

COLUMBIA UNIVERSITY PRESS   NEW YORK

The cover art is a charcoal drawing, "Germination,"
by Odilon Redon. From a private collection.

Columbia University Press
New York   Oxford
Copyright © 1989 Columbia University Press
All rights reserved

LIBRARY OF CONGRESS
Library of Congress Cataloging-in-Publication Data

McGrane, Bernard
Beyond anthropology: society and the other / Bernard McGrane.
p.   cm.
Bibliography: p.
Includes index.
ISBN 0-231-06684-8
ISBN 0-231-06685-6 (pbk.)
1. Anthropology—Philosophy—History.   2. Difference (Philosophy)
3. Ethnocentrism.   4. Social perception—History.
5. Man (Christian theology)   I. Title
GN33M34 1989
306'.09—dc19
88.22886
CIP

Printed in the United States of America

Casebound editions of Columbia University Press books are Smyth-sewn
and printed on permanent and durable acid-free paper.

c 10 9 8 7 6 5 4 3 2 1
p 10 9 8 7 6 5 4 3 2 1

In gratitude to those teachers who taught me to think: Walter Petry, Alan Blum, and Richard Sennett; and to Ronnie and Jonathan.

CONTENTS

PREFACE

We have only to speak of an object to think that we are being objective. But, because we chose it in the first place, the object reveals more about us than we do about it.

Gaston Bachelard

We see the world the way we do not because that is the way it is but because we have these ways of seeing.

Ludwig Wittgenstein

This work is an inquiry into the history of the different conceptions of difference from roughly the sixteenth to the early twentieth century. A culture which "discovers" that which is alien to itself also thereby fundamentally reveals that which it is to itself. Within the organization of knowledge in the sixteenth century, in Renaissance cosmography, the alienness of the non-European Other was experienced and interpreted on the horizon of Christianity. It was Christianity which fundamentally came between the European and the non-European Other. Within the Christian conception of Otherness anthropology did not exist; there was, rather, demonology. It was in relation to the Fall and to the influence of Sin and Satan that the Other took on his historically specific meaning.

[handwritten margin note: ✓ but, the other existed in antiquity]

In the Enlightenment organization of knowledge, the general paradigm for interpreting and explaining the foreignness of the non-European Other underwent a fundamental reorganization and it was Ignorance which came between the European and the Other. Anthropology did not exist: there was, rather, an Enlightenment psychology of error and superstition, an ontology of ignorance, and an epistemology of all the forms of untruth and unenlightenment. It was upon the surface and the administration of this historical horizon that the Other assumed his general form and specific meaning.

In the nineteenth century the general interpretive paradigm altered once again: there occurred a vast hemorrage in time: geological time, evolutionary time, developmental time lodged itself between the European and the non-European Other. Anthropology came into being. It organized and administered the comparison between past and present, between different "stages of development," between the prehistorically fossilized "primitive" and the evolutionary advancement of modern Western science and civilization. As the general ontological status and theological significance of the "animal" undergoes a profound transformation with Darwin's *Origin of the Species* (1859), so, analogously, does the status and significance of the non-European Other in Tylor's *Primitive Culture* (1871). The non-Eurpoean Other became the positive form of an evolution.

In the early twentieth century, finally, the authoritative paradigm for interpreting and explaining the difference of the Other undergoes a mutation once again and now, for us, "Culture" accounts for the difference of the Other. We think under the hegemony of the ethnological response to the alienness of the Other; we are, today, contained within an anthropological concept of the Other. Anthropology has become our modern way of seeing the Other as, both fundamentally and merely, culturally different.

In *The Order of Things,* Foucault says: "Anthropology constitutes perhaps the fundamental arrangement that has governed and controlled the path of philosophical thought from Kant until our own day. This arrangement is essential since it forms part of our history; but it is disintegrating before our eyes since we are beginning to recognize and denounce in it, in a critical mode, both the forgetfulness of the opening that made it possible and a stubborn obstacle standing obstinately in the way of an immanent new form of thought. To all those who still wish to talk about man . . . who wish to take him as their starting point in their attempts to reach the truth . . . who refer all knowledge back to the truths of man himself . . . who refuse to think without immediately thinking that it is man who is thinking, to all these warped and twisted forms of reflection, we can answer only with a philosophical laugh. . . . One thing in any case is certain; man is neither the oldest nor the most constant problem that has been posed for human knowledge. Taking a relatively short chronological sample within a restricted geographical area—European culture since the sixteenth century—one can be certain that man is a recent invention within it. It is not around him and his secrets that knowledge prowled for so long in the darkness. In fact, among all the mutations that have affected the knowledge of things and their order . . . only one, that which began a century and a half ago and is now perhaps drawing to a close, has made it possible for the figure of man to appear . . . if those arrangements were to disappear as they appeared, if some event of which we can at the moment do no more than sense the possibility . . . were to cause them to crumble . . . then one can certainly wager that man would be erased, like a face drawn in sand at the edge of the sea."

BEYOND ANTHROPOLOGY

INTRODUCTION

Well we all need someone we can dream on.
The Rolling Stones

Foucault maintains, in his archaeology of the human sciences, that an "archaeological mutation" in the groundwork of Western knowledge at the dawn of the nineteenth century brought about the appearance of "man": "man" as the subject matter, as the ground and horizon of the "human sciences"; "man" as that over-powering configuration in the space of our knowledge the existence of whom we can only with the utmost effort doubt. Foucault sees himself as raising the question

. . .which may well seem aberrant, so opposed is it to what has rendered the whole of our thought historically possible. The question would be: Does man really exist? To imagine, for an instant what the world and thought and truth might be if man did not exist, is considered to be merely indulging in paradox. This is because we are so blinded by the recent man-ifestation of man that we can no longer remember a time—and it is not so long ago—when the world, its order, and hu-man beings existed but man did not. (Foucault 1970:322)

This essay, under the haunting specter of Foucault's question, is a small attempt at an "archaeology of anthropology" using, for the most part, the methods devised by him in his "archaeology of knowledge," together with the methods and concerns of "ethno-methodology" as originated by Harold Garfinkel and developed by Alan Blum. I am writing a history of the different conceptions of "alien cutlures" from roughly the sixteenth to the early twentieth century. A culture that discovers what is alien to itself simulta-neously manifests what it is in itself. "The European's images of

1

non-European man are not primarily, if at all, descriptions of real people, but rather projections of this own nostalgia and feeling of inadequacy. They are judgments on himself and his history" (Baudet 1965:vii). This work attempts to chart the transformations of a perpetually present identity crisis in reference to the Other. Perhaps somewhat analogous to Trotski's notion of a permanent revolution I attempt to chart this "field" as a permanent crisis in identity, a continuous identity anxiety. The history of anthropology is the history of an identity crisis, and a history of the different identities we have existed.

James Joyce says somewhere that art isn't *about* anything; it *is* something. Similarly, I attempt to treat anthropology as fundamentally not being "about" anything, but rather as being something. This treatment of the history of anthropology is based on an ethnomethodologically inspired theoretical commitment of sustained indifference toward the conventionally presumed realism of anthropology and ethnographic description; and one of my principal questions, analogous to Foucault's questioning of "man" is "Does culture really exist?." This version of the history of anthropology strives to participate in that "fundamental reconceptualization of European intellectual history" laid out by Foucault's archaeological studies that

> not only comprehend the other human sciences, in the sense of transcending and explaining them; they point as well to the dissolution of belief in the "positivity" of such concepts as "man," "society," and "culture." Structuralism signals, in Foucault's judgment, the discovery by Western thought of the linguistic basis of such concepts as "man," "society," and "culture," the discovery that these concepts refer, not to things, but to linguistic formulae that have no specific referents in reality. (White 1973:24)

In writing an archaeology of anthropology, a history of the different conceptions of difference, I am concerned with making visible, in reference to European self-understanding, the Other, the Other as non-European. This is an attempt not to understand the Other, the alien, the different, but rather, historically, to understand our understanding of the Other, the alien, the different. Philosophically, the frame of reference guiding this study is the aspiration to recognize the Other as empty, i.e., empty of our

2

conceptions, empty of our projections. In reference to the Other, we need to become aware of our projections, not deceived by them. I am engaged therefore in writing a history of the changing structure of projections; a history that goes against the grain of the conventional positivist impulse and project to objectify reality and hence to objectify the Other, to objectify our reactions to the Other and the otherness of the Other.

By the nineteenth century "anthropology" became, to a large degree, a discursive practice whose systematic administrative function was to maintain belief in the existence of exotic and alien worlds without fusing the alien with our world. It became exactly, in this respect, terrestrial science fiction, dealing with terrestrial aliens, as indeed, science fiction soon became extraterrestrial anthropology, dealing with extraterrestrial aliens (Philmus 1970). There is a great similarity, from an archaeological perspective, between what we term modern "anthropological discourse" and what we term modern "science fiction": for with the non-European Other as with the aliens-from-other-planets, what is significant is not whether such beings exist or not, but, rather, *the fact that they are conceivable.* I'm not interested in the fact and nature of their existence, but I'm very much interested in the fact and nature of their conceivability. For example, I'm not interested in when the "primitive" or "paleolithic man" was discovered, but when and under what conditions the "primitive" or "paleolithic man" became conceivable.

This essay intends, hopefully, to be a contribution to the historical and critical self-understanding of anthropology. Though at times I somewhat unreflexively treat anthropologists as "primitives" (i.e., I do an anthropology of anthropologist's beliefs as they do anthropological studies of primitive's beliefs), more generally I treat the history of anthropology as a structuralist literary historian might treat the history of science fiction; that is, in the same way that a literary historian could not treat science fiction as a concrete description of anything, so I do not treat anthropology as a concrerte description of anything. There are no independently existing "science fiction" beings available over against which the various historical modes of science fiction writing, and the various historical images thereby produced may be compared with for the sake of positivistically evaluating their descriptive accuracy and adequacy—their "truth." The various figures and landscapes of science fiction are not discovered and described, but invented and

3

constructed: during the Middle Ages and Renaissance, in a specifically hierarchic cosmos (Cassirer 1963), these figures and landscapes were versions of and variations on "angles and demons"; during the Enlightenment, in an astonishingly uniform and profoundly homogenous universe (Cassirer 1955, Lovejoy 1936) they became versions of and variations on "men" and "civilized beings" and, in the nineteenth and twentieth centuries they became, in accordance with a biological, deeply Darwinian universe (Cassirer 1950), "Martians" and "alien life forms." They are not, and never have been, things described. Likewise, I treat historical versions of "anthropology" as imaginatively possible worlds (somewhat as Foucault treated "psychiatry" in *Madness and Civilization*), and the beings it speaks of I treat as grounded in the historically changing forms—paradigms in Kuhn's sense—of anthropological discourse and practice. Anthropology, in short, does not simply describe its subject matter; it systematically constructs and produces it. Hence I seek, in a historical manner, to redissolve and deconstruct the non-European Other back into the record of the choices made in creating him as a subject for imagination and thought. (Indeed the very use of "him" as a pronoun for the Other is itself reflective of historical choices—perhaps a sort of subconscious symbolic annihilation of women, a grammatic-discursive gendercide.)

That the concrete prior existence of other cultures—"primitive cultures"—was the necessary and sufficient condition for the possibility, emergence, rise, and history of what we now call "anthropology" is an approach I do not intend to pursue. That approach seems to me grounded in the positivistic faith:[1] in the belief that the criterion of the truth and the historical progress and perfection of our scientific theories lies in their ever closer approximation to an autonomous reality. The prior and autonomous existence of what we call "primitive cultures" was not the "stimulus" for anthropology, and the emergence out of the matrix and density of the Western tradition of what we call "anthropology" was not the subsequent "response" naturalistically dictated by that stimulus. Rather, the historical emergence and course of what we call "anthropology"—the theoretical treatment of "primitive cultures"— and the historical emergence and course of what we call "primitive cultures" are two ways of looking at the same thing:

In order to claim that primitive societies (or whatever replaces them now as the object of anthropology) are the reality and

4

our conceptualizations the theory, one must keep anthropology standing on its head. If we can show that our theories of their societies are *our praxis*—the way in which we produce and reproduce knowledge of the Other for our societies—we may . . . put anthropology back on its feet. Renewed interest in the history of our discipline and disciplined inquiry into the history of confrontation between anthropology and its Other are therefore . . . ways to meet the Other on the same ground, in the same Time. (Fabian 1983:165)

Analytically, the desire of every "rational practice" is to cultivate and make reference to its reason for existence (Blum 1974). Hence, from this perspective, the decisive feature of anthropology is not the concrete state-of-affairs it speaks about, but rather the reason for its speech and the context, conditions and possibility of its speech. Its interest is itself, its being, and the maintenance of the conditions of its possibility (or, as Marx would say, the reproduction of the conditions of production). Its subject matter is concretely "primitive cultures"; analytically, itself. Anthropology as a contemporary discursive practice having a disciplinary identity has become institutionalized (Stocking 1987): as such it is an institution fundamentally involved in the reproduction of Western society. Anthropology as the organized treatment of an exterior alterity (Levinas 1969) is, I believe, a supreme manifestation of the Western tradition. It manifests and highlights that egocentric tendency of our Western mind to identify itself as separate from what it perceives as external to itself. In its analytic structure, it is concerned with and reveals more about itself and its matrix the Western tradition, than any of the concrete "primitive cultures" it concretely studies. The *invention of culture* (Wagner 1975), via the recognition and construction of other cultures, marked a monumental event in the Western tradition. That invention is the subject of this study.

5

I

THE OTHER
IN THE RENAISSANCE

The discovery of America, or of the Americans, is certainly the most astonishing encounter of our history. We do not have the same sense of radical difference in the "discovery" of other continents and of other peoples: Europeans have never been altogether ignorant of the existence of Africa, India, or China; some memory of these places was always there from the beginning . . . it is in fact the conquest of America that heralds and establishes our present identity. . . . The entire history of the discovery of America, the first episode of the conquest, is marked by this ambiguity: human alterity is at once revealed and rejected.

> Tzvetan Todorov
> The Conquest of America

In the documents of the sixteenth century, how does the Other become a subject for imagination and thought and an object of practical action? How does the difference and otherness of the Other become stabilized into an object of discourse? How does he become captured by speech and imprisoned in knowledge? What conditions must the Other conform to in order to become describeable? How does the Other become known? And, in relation to what is the Other understood? What appears in proximity to the Other and can be related to him? What does not appear? (What does *not* appear in relation to the Other as non-European is Progress, the progress of knowledge and science, the nature and ascent, or decline, of History and Civilization, and the Origin of Society, as in the nineteenth century; nor again, Culture, and the visible-grounds-for-maintaining-a-possible-pluralistic-relativism-in-regard-to-the-cultural-foundations-of-all-knowledge-and-behavior, as in the twentieth century.) In the sixteenth century that discourse which systematically forms itself and grows around the strangeness and alienness of the Other, the non-European Other, is termed cosmography. In sixteenth-century cosmography—in Peter Martyr,

7

in Sebastian Munster, in Christopher Columbus, in Amerigo Vespucci, in Gonsalo Vernandez de Oviedo, Jose de Acosta, in Johannes Boemus, in Bartolome de Las Casa, in Richard Hakluyt—three principle "objects" appear in propinquity to the Other as non-European. These three "objects" and their illusive interplay are formative in reference to the fundamental mode of being that the Other is to assume in the sixteenth century: firstly, the demonic, the Christian demonic; secondly, the Ancients, especially the Greeks; and thirdly, gold-and-spices. It is by charting these three objects and the space, the common locus, that grounds and makes possible their intellectual juxtaposition and the play of their interrelationships that we may determine how, in the sixteenth century, the otherness of the non-European Other becomes an object of discourse and imagination, and the subject matter of a discipline.[1]

MONSTERS AND GEOGRAPHY

"In fine, this may we boldly affirm, that the antiquity had never such knowledge of the world which the sun compasseth about in twenty-four hours as we have at this present by the industry of the men of this our age" (Arber 1885:247). So wrote Richard Eden in 1555 by way of preface to the seaman Antonio Pigafetta's account of his voyage with Magellan around the world.[2] The Medieval possibility of unconsciously experiencing a direct and uniform continuity with the Ancients' cosmography and geography with all their bizarre peoples, places and monsters is permanently shattered. In 1519 Maximelian Transilvane reported that the survivors of Magellan's heroic voyage

gave the selfsame information both to the emperor's majesty and diverse others: and this with such faithfulness and sincerity, that not only they are judged of all men to have declared the truth in all things, but have thereby also given us certain knowledge that all that hath hitherto been said or written of old authors as touching those things are false and fabulous. For who will believe that men are found with only one leg? Or with such feet whose shadow covereth their bodies. Or men of a cubic height, and other such like being rather monsters than men? Of the which, neither the Spainyards, who

8

in our time sailing by the ocean sea, have discovered all the coasts of the lands toward the west . . . nor the Portugals who compassing about Africa have passed by all the East . . . nor yet the Spainyards in their last navigation, in which they compassed about the whole earth, did never in any of their voyages write of such monsters: which doubtless they would not have omitted if they might have had certain knowledge thereof. (Arber 1885:248)

A new and specifically modern sense of verisimilitude is slowly formed and assumes authoritative dominance over geographical statements. The unity, coherence, and centrality of the geography established by Ptolemy, by Strabo, and by Pliny is permanently dislocated. Certain pivotal statements and credences that hitherto had been held as true and acceptable become, suddenly, not false and disproved—as do other statements previously held as true— but rather are now seen to fall wholly outside the threshold of sensible bounds, outside the parameters of normal, authoritative geographical discourse.

What comes to the fore in reference to traditional cosmographical knowledge is, at first sight, the simple "empirical erroneousness" of the ancient authors as revealed by the "empirical voyages of discovery." A closer look, however, reveals that sixteenth-century cosmography does not experience itself as progressing beyond the limited cosmography of the ancients, but rather as breaking with this tradition, a past, that it now experiences not so much as false, erroneous, but rather as fabulous and fantastic, as a teratology. More than seeing antiquity as making erroneous and false statements, sixteenth-century cosmography sees the ancients as often making monstrous statements, especially in their statements about monsters. A discipline such as geography is not essentially definable merely by the group of true statements it makes about its subject matter. It is also essentially composed of the acceptable errors it makes and makes possible. The acceptably false is what is recognizable and identifiable; thus erroneous and invalid statements are still part of the discipline. Outside the discipline, however, prowl "monstrosities" and monstrous statements. These seem to be outside the administration of the authoritative paradigm, outside the respectable parameters; they are wild, undisciplined statements that nevertheless seem somehow relevant, somehow

9

distant relatives, but yet they cannot be fitted, cannot be true or false. A good segment of the traditional geographical discourse of the ancients—Ptolemy's *Geography* (1932), Strabo's *Geography* (1932), Pliny's *Natural History* (1956), Pomponius Mela's *Di situ orbis* (1590), Solinus' *De mirabilibus mundi* (1587), and Herodotus (1942), and Mandeville (1964), and Isadore of Seville (Brehaut 1912)[3]—is seen by sixteenth-century cosmography as invalid, but such that it is composed of acceptable and accepted errors. The invalidity of these segments, for example Herodotus and Pliny's error as to the original source of cinnamon (Arber 1895:247), is a valid invalidity. Another large segment of this traditional corpus of geographical knowledge of the Ancients, however, suddenly cannot be related to given the new voyages of discovery. What had been Jekyll suddenly becomes Hyde.

The geographical imagination has been permanently altered; the nature of geographical space has been permanently transformed, and with that transformation the nature of the possible objects that can be discovered, located and deployed in that space undergo an equally deep transformation. For the geographical discourse of the sixteenth century the Age of Monsters is dead, and, by a strange irony, the now bizarre-looking geography of the Ancients becomes the only true monster it recognizes. Now what is truly monstrous is the old, fantastic, truly monstrous *form* of ignorance that believed in monsters.

THE OTHER MANIFESTS THE INFERNAL

"Satan has now been expelled from the island . . . his influence has disappeared now that most of the Indians are dead. . . . Who can deny that the use of gunpowder against pagans is the burning of incense to Our Lord" (Oviedo). In the cosmography of the sixteenth century the Other is related to the Christianity he lacks, the clothes he doesn't wear, the gold he doesn't want, the iron he doesn't have, the written alphabet he doesn't use. But above all to Christianity. He is pagan rather than heretic. The Other in the sixteenth century is, precisely, a non-Christian, dwelling entirely in the hollow of absence, the inscribed inhabitant of an inverted space. The key to understanding this first idea of the alienness of the Other is understanding how this figure was constructed by a systematic thought-process of inversion.

10

If anyone wonder at some fashions and customs of the Indies, and will scorne them as fooles, or abhorre them as divelish and inhumane people, let him remember that the same things, yea, worse, have been seen amongst the Greeks and Romans . . . as we may easily understand not only of our authors, as Eusebius of Caesarea, Clement of Alexandria, and others, but also of their owne, as Plinie, Dionysius of Halicarnaus, and Plutarke: for the Prince of darkness being the head of all Infidelitie, it is no new thing to find among Infidells, cruelties, filthines, and follies fit for such a master. (de Acosta 1890:296)

In the cosmographical discourse of the sixteenth century the non-European Other cannot be related to nor understood apart from the Christian Devil. Duran gives us another instance:

On the other hand, one *can* say that the devil had persuaded and instructed them, stealing from and imitating the Divine Cult so that *he* be honored as a god; for everything was a mixture of a thousand heathen beliefs, deceits, and imperfections. . . . Either (as I have said) our Holy Christian Religion was known in this land, or the devil our cursed adversary forced the Indians to imitate the ceremonies of the Christian Catholic religion in his own service and cult, being thus adored and served. (Quoted in Todorov 1984:210)

The central preoccupation with reference to the Other in the sixteenth century is whether he is within the threshold of salvation, of conversion, or, whether he is beyond hope: it is within the context of this question that his degree of humanity (sameness) will be determined. "If he was not a man, then he was incapable of receiving the faith" (de Acosta). "What is certain is that all these people are our brothers, proceeding from Adam's stock even as we ourselves" (Sahagun). Using this capacity for conversion as a criterion, Paul III proclaimed in the bull *Sublimis Deus* of 1537 that "the Indians are true men." Thus the process of inversion is the background upon which the preoccupation with conversion emerges as the decisive referent for delimiting and understanding the otherness of the Other.

Francisco de Vitoria, one of the pinnacles of Spainish humanism in the sixteenth century, writes, "Although these barbarians are not altogether mad . . . yet they are not far from being

11

so. . . . They are not, or are no longer, capable of governing themselves any more than madmen or even wild beasts and animals. . . . Their stupidity is much greater than that of . . . madmen in other countries" (quoted in Todorov 1984:150). The sixteenth-century non-European, like the sixteenth-century madman, cannot be understood apart from the Fall (Foucault 1965). But the myth of the Fall complicates this construction of the Other by inversion. Man, i.e., European man, needs redemption because in the beginning he committed an original sin. Are aliens pre-sin, like Adam, or are they outside the geography of these terms? If conversion does not work, then they too, like the European, must have committed a primal crime of their own—but then they aren't alien. As sinners who seek to redeem themselves they lose, in the minds of the European observer, their non-European distinctiveness. An early cosmographer and governor on one of the isles of the West Indies, Oviedo, recurs again and again to this problem. In his *Natural History of the West Indies* (1526) he writes of the diabolical practices and rites of the natives. After describing one instance of how a certain "priestly sect" is periodically summoned by the native king to divine the future by allowing themselves for a short time to be possessed by a spirit, Oviedo goes on, "But since the Christian faith hath been dispersed throughout the island these devilish practices have ceased, and they of the members of the devil are made the members of Christ by baptism, forsaking the devil and his works, with the vain curiosity of desire of knowledge of things to come, whereof for the most part it is better to be ignorant than with vexation to know that which cannot be avoided" (Oviedo 1959:87). Oviedo displays in this instance a concern analogous to that previously heard in the analyses of madness. It is an old theme, lying at the heart of the Christian drama of life, concerned with the vanity of knowledge. From the perspective of Christian values, the esoteric alchemist, the early Faust, as the incarnation of the pride and vanity of knowledge, is seen as punished by madness for the too ardent, the too immoderate desire (lust) for too much knowledge. Referring to the sixteenth century Foucault says,

> No doubt, madness has something to do with the strange paths
> of knowledge. The first canto of Brant's poem is devoted to
> books and scholars. . . . But if knowledge is so important to
> madness, it is not because the latter can control the secrets of

12

knowledge; on the contrary, madness is the punishment of a disorderly and useless science. If madness is the truth of knowledge, it is because knowledge is absurd. . . . (Foucault 1965:25)

Let us consider further the comparisons of the Other as heathen savage and the madman. For sixteenth-century cosmography, the diabolical is not yet, as it would later become, an autonomous, independent perpetually contradicting antiworld, horribly and absurdly incapable of submitting to a rational or emotional explanation. The alien is also defined by inversion, but then, in his very sinfulness, he also becomes a brother. He is still very much thereby an emotionally and intellectually intelligible segment within the Christian cosmos. In its often grotesque portrait of the Other's necessary yet culpable complicity with the Infernal, sixteenth-century cosmography still participates in the fundamentally coherent unity of Bosch's cosmos rather than in the fundamentally incoherent discontinuity of Bruegel's chaos.

It is with good reason that the eighteenth century considered Bruegel to be more grotesque than Bosch, and that its definition of the concept of the grotesque was based on Bruegel's paintings. Bruegel decisively breaks with the tradition, according to which the infernal world forms a part of the Christian cosmos. He does not paint a Christian hell, whose monsters serve as God's tools in warning, tempting, or punishing, but an absurd nocturnal world of its own which permits of no rational or emotional explanation. (Kayser 1963:36)

Hell's nocturnal world is still a part of the Christian day, and the Devil and the ways of the Devil are still God's instruments, participating, however obliquely and indirectly, in His administration and His government.

There is never, in cosmography, a question or anxiety about the power of contagion, in reference to the non-European and the non-Christian way of life. In the otherness of the madman and of madness there is a perpetually present and haunting fear of contagion, as in the terrifying visions of Bruegel, Dürer, Bosch, and Grunwald, or Sebastian Brant's epic poem *Narrenschiff* (Ship of Fools). With the Other as savage there is never the possibility of invasion. The fundamental European response to this alien Other lies in the massive and ceaseless task of conversion. The subterranean point of linkage between the madman and the non-Christian Other in the sixteenth century is the Devil, in that the madman is a sign of the Infernal, obscurely linked to the Fall and Punishment, and the non-Christian Other is, per force, in complicity with the Devil and likewise obscurely linked to the Fall and Punishment. As one of the great sympathetic preservers of the Indian traditions, Bernardo de Sahagun writes,

> "You, inhabitants of this New Spain . . . know that you have lived in the great darkness of idolatry and faithlessness in which your ancestors have left you, as is proved clearly in your writings, your drawings, and the idolatrous rites in which you have lived until this day. . . . " Following then with a vivid description of child sacrifice enacted by the Indians Sahagun continues, "The cause of this cruel blinding, of which these wretched children were the object, must not so much be imputed to the cruelty of their fathers, who were shedding abundant tears and indulging in such practises with pain in their hearts; *we must impute it to the infinitely cruel hatred of our ancient enemy Satan.*" (Ouoted in Todorov 1984, emphasis mine)

THE OTHER AS POTENTIAL CHRISTIAN

"They have no religion, nor are they idolators" (Columbus). For cosmography and for that newly emergent form of discourse that later came to be known as "travel literature," the object of discourse in the sixteenth century is the non-Christian. "The line between the Christian and the Muslim was clearly drawn and their normal relation was war" (Parry 1961:69). In the "Age of Exploration" as over against the preceding "Age of Crusades," the Other is not anti-Christian, as the ever threatening Moors had been, but *non-Christian*. This non-Christian is also a *potential* Christian. (These savages are, similarly, potential Europeans, and from this comes the primal practice of *naming* the "territories" discovered: what does Spain "discover" after all but "New Spain," and France "New France," and England "New England.") In the papal bull of 1537 Paul III declares that the Indians are "true men," capable of receiving the Christian faith and that, essentially, they are "equal" to European Christians. As Todorov says,

14

This declaration *derives from* fundamental Christian principles; . . . Las Casas therefore adopts this position and gives
it a more general expression, positing equality as the basis of
all human policy, "The natural laws and rules and rights of
men are common to all nations, Christian and gentile and
whatever their sect, law, state, color and condition, without
any difference. . . . All the Indians to be found here are to be
held as free; for in truth they are so, by the same right as I
myself am free. . . . " *But this very declaration of the equality
of men is made in the name of a specific religion, Christianity,*
though without this specifically being acknowledged. (Todorov
1984:162, emphasis mine).

Somewhere between war and peace, the non-Christian will essentially not be regarded as being in possession of a competing
reality. In their commercial exploration of India and the east Vasco
da Gama's men "even confused Hindus with Christians; at least
they were prepared to regard all who were not Muslims as potential Christians" (Parry 1961:95). Thus the Other is defined by a
double movement, by a rule of exclusion that incorporated him.
Further, whereas the Muslim contradicts Christianity (Europe), the
New World savages are seen as potential Christians. In the "Age
of Crusades" the Other had been the anti-Christ, and he left no
room for expansion. In these sixteenth-century voyages, the act of
exploration takes on a new meaning: the world will henceforth serve
as the blank canvas for the greatest Christianization in history. Las
Casas in his *History of the Indies* (1527–1560) maintains that the
significance of Columbus was that he was "the first who opened
the doors of this Ocean Sea, through which he entered and introduced to these so remote lands and realms, until then so unknown,
our Savior Jesus Christ" (Las Casas 1971a:37). Also de Oviedo, who,
while recalling the famous statues that antiquity created of its
heros, insists, in his *Natural History of the West Indies* (1526), that
Columbus is worthy of a like honor; "As a brave and wise sailor,
and a courageous captain, he showed to us this New World, which
is so full of gold that thousands of such statues could have been
made out of the gold that is sent to Spain. But he is still worthy
of fame and glory for having brought the Catholic faith to these
parts" (Oviedo 1959:29).
For sixteenth-century cosmography the non-Europeans are per-

15

ceived as dwelling within the clear, limpid, and neutral space of potentiality, having essentially and necessarily no density of their own, no possible "religion" of their own, as in nineteenth century anthropology. For in the sixteenth century *there is Christianity but there is no "religion."* Religion is not yet the genus of which "Christianity" will be merely a species; this intellectual movement and way of seeing does not occur until the Enlightenment. Tillich perhaps captures this best when he says,

> The leaders of the Enlightenment, Locke, Hume, and Kant, measured Christianity by its reasonableness and judged all other religions by the same criterion. . . . These ideas inspired a large number of Protestant theologians in the nineteenth century and early twentieth century. A symptom of this situation is the rise of philosophies of religion, the very term implying that Christianity has been subsumed under the universal concept of religion. . . . This seems harmless enough, but it is not . . . since the concept of religion is itself derived from the Christian-humanist tradition the procedure is circular. (Tillich 1963:41–43)

On this horizon of concern then, the savages represent human nature devoid of the organizing presence of Christianity. The non-Europeans bear witness to the fact that for sixteenth-century cosmography nature is not natural as it would be for nineteenth-century anthropology, but rather "fallen," "demonical," not a neutral space but a black and void backdrop, not an essentially lawful determinism but an essentially limitless darkness. Peter Martyr, in his *Decades of the New World,* written intermittently as letters between 1493 and 1530, explains the difference of these non-Europeans.

> You shall now therefore understand the illusions wherewith the people of the island Hispaniola have been seduced after the errors of the old gentilitie, and wandered in the ignorance and blindness of human nature corrupted by the disobedience of our first parents, which hath remained in all nations upon the face of the earth, except where it hath pleased God by the light of his spirit by his word, to pour upon his elect the grace of renovation, by the light whereof the natural darkness receiveth some clearness as in a glass, until imperfection shall be abolished. (Arber 1885:189)

16

For cosmography the natural world of the non-European, and by implication, nature itself, had no inner rationale: even their languages appeared more as a brute piece of unintelligible nature than as a sensible expression of Christian humanity:

In a memorandum drawn up for the ecclastical counsel of 1585 Dr. Oritz de Hinojosa of the University of Mexico described some of the languages of New Spain as being so inaccessible and difficult that they appear to have been introduced not by men but by nature, as the illiterate noise of birds or brute animals, which cannot be written down with any kind of character, and can scarcely be pronounced for being so guttural that they stick in the throat. (Elliott 1972:16)

Those who like to write about the "ethnography" of the sixteenth-century explorers, sailors, missionaries, and cosmographers overlook the small yet decisive fact that "ethnography" did not exist. The description of the "manners" and "customs" of foreign peoples, of aliens, of savages, did not exist. The "manners" and "customs" of these peoples were not experienced as being instances of primitive behavior or instances of different cultures, as in nineteenth-century anthropology. Rather their actions and behavior were experienced as being manifestations of barbarism and savage degeneracy—a hybrid composite of Christian "nature" and Christian "evil." The ethnographic description of "primitive peoples" embedded in nineteenth-century positivism presupposes the desire to literally transcribe and report the "reality" of the Other, to acquire "objective" knowledge (observations) of the Other. By contrast, Pigafetta, one of the few surviving sailors who successfully completed that grueling, herioc voyage around the world under Magellan, writes;

When the Captain demanded of him [the native king of the Pacific Island of Zubut] why all the idols on the island were not burnt according to his promise, he answered thay they esteemed them no more as gods, but only made sacrifice to them for the Prince's brother who was very sick. . . . The Captain answered that if he would burn all his idols and believe faithfully in Christ and be baptized, he should be immediately restored to his health, and that he would else give them leave to strike off his head. By these words and persuasions of the Captain, he conceived such hope of health that after he was

17

baptized he felt no more grief of his disease. And this was a manifest miracle wrought in our time whereby diverse infidels were converted to our faith and their idols destroyed and also their altars overthrown on the which they were accustomed to eat the sacrifical flesh. (Arber 1885;257)

What we have in sixteenth-century cosmography and travel literature is not the perception of "customs" on the horizon of the acquisition of positive knowledge, but rather perception of strategies on the horizon of the vanquishing of false faiths. "Missionaries need precise information on pagan superstitions if they were to cast down the idolaters. 'To preach against those things,' wrote Sahagun, 'and even to know if they exist, it is necessary to know how they used them in the time of their idolatry'"(Elliott 1972:6). Again, "It was religion, more than trade, more even than the needs of secular administration, that forced Europeans to understand how other peoples lived and thought" (Hale 1967:342).

Notice the peculiar consequence of this way of seeing the world. The barbarians' "customs" are not seen as "indigenous customs" in the ethnographic sense.

The religious were not interested in studying native society for its own sake, but only as a means of incorporating it as quickly and as completely as possible into what Oviedo called "the Christian Republic." Given their overriding determination to extirpate abominable and idolatrous practices, it was natural that sympathetic understanding of native civilization should stop abruptly at those points where the Indians had surrendered themselves irrevocably to the devil and his works. Christianity, for instance, precluded a dispassionate approach to the problem of cannibalism. . . . (Elliott 1970:34)

This is why, only *after* the project and the experience *of conversion* could the alien be considered *in relation to the acquisition of knowledge*. Only then could "ethnography" as a positive discipline emerge: as signposted by Feuerbach, only after Christianity comes Anthropology.

Further, the customs, especially the horrifying customs, of the savages were not seen as something requiring explanation. Insofar as these savages and their customs could be seen as instancing or signifying something other than themselves, they were seen as representing the "naturally" degenerate, the natural degeneracy of

18

nature, rather than the historically primitive; they represented man in a Fallen rather than a primitive form.

It was hardly necessary to probe much further into Indian belief systems or social behavior for explanations of cannibalism and human sacrifice when such horrible rites were known to be inherent in the condition of paganism itself. The heathen, as Acosta pointed out, were by virtue of their paganism slaves to the prince of darkness, and prone, in consequence, to every form of evil. (Elliott 1972:23)

NAMING AND CHRISTENING

Let us return to the issue of naming. Its importance as a primary practice can now perhaps be more fully seen. After seventy arduous and often terror filled days of sailing, on October 12, 1492 (according to our Western chronology), Columbus came upon land. After a short reconnaissance he determined that he had landed on an island that, together with some other small islands, was situated in all probability off the coast of Cipangu (Japan). One island he called "Hispaniola" and the other he called "Johanna." On his second voyage Columbus arrived at a different island, "and because he came thither on the Sunday called the Dominical day, he called the island where he arrived, Dominica. He passed also innumerable other islands which he named, as Mons Harratus, Santa Maria rotunda, Sancta Martinus, Sancta Maria Antiqua and Sancta Cruz" (Arber 1885:30).

The implicit sovereignty of giving names, of nomination, has a historically specific character in the sixteenth century. Pigafetta, a sailor with Magellan, writes;

The Sunday following, the king was baptized with great solemnity. . . . After this, the captain caused them to break the idols and set up the cross in diverse places. . . . The king in his baptism was named Charles after the emperor's name, and the Prince, Ferdinando, after the name of his majesty's brother. The king of Messana was named John and the Moor Christopher. To all others they gave names as are commonly used in Christendom. (Arber 1885:257)

In the sixteenth century names did not name in a neutral sense, nor did they function as naming in a geographical sense, rather,

19

fundamentally, *names Christened*. To name was to Christianize and to Baptize. Only in relation to the horizon of conversion can sixteenth-century cosmography's worldwide giving of names be understood. Todorov, in *The Conquest of America* also notes this:

> Like Adam in the midst of Eden, Columbus is profoundly concerned with the choices of names for the virgin world before his eyes. . . . Columbus knows perfectly well that these islands already have names . . . however he seeks to rename places . . . to give them the *right* names; moreover nomination is equivalent to taking possession. . . . The first gesture Columbus makes upon contact with the newly discovered lands (hence the first contact between Europe and what will be America) is an act of extended nomination: this is the declaration according to which these lands are henceforth part of the Kingdom of Spain. . . . That this should be the very first action performed by Columbus in America tells us a great deal about the importance the ceremony of naming assumed in his eyes. (Todorov 1984:26–28)

THE GREEK AND THE SAVAGE: THE REDISCOVERY OF THE ANCIENT WORLD AND THE DISCOVERY OF THE NEW WORLD

In Peter Martyr's epistolary book *The Decades of the New World*, the "descriptions" of the various practices and customs, especially the "religious" rites, of the inhabitants of the New World are permeated with references to Ancient Greek customs. In one respect the cosmographical discourse of the sixteenth century was constituted by arranging the inhabitants of the New World and the Ancient Greeks on the same horizon. They were both figures at the far edges, the parameters, of the Christian cosmos. This equating of the two produced some, to us, odd results.

The customs of the Ancient Greeks were used as an analogical elucidation of the practices of the inhabitants of the New World. "In order to describe the Indians the conquistadors seek comparisons they find immediately . . . in their own pagan (Greco-Roman) past" (Todorov 1984:108). Yet Christian faith proclaimed native custom to be meaningless, except as a species of evil. And further, the customs of the Ancient Greeks were now seen in their

20

turn to be elucidated by the practices of the New Worlders. The aliens of the present—the savages—were seen as elucidating and being elucidated by the aliens of the past—the Greeks. Strange geography and strange time have a common referent. Martyr, in a letter to an Italian prince, says, after describing how some of the native priests sniff a certain herbal powder that induces violent hallucinations, howlings and furious outpourings that are taken to be prophecies, "Now most noble prince what need you hereafter marvel at the spirit of Apollo so shaking his Sibylles with extreme fury? You had thought that the superstitious antiquitie had perished" (Arber 1885:102).

But the relationship is more complicated. In the cosmography of the sixteenth century, statements about the Greeks and statements about the inhabitants of the New World coexist. Columbus' company, Martyr relates, was taken to "a great island which the captives that were taken in Hispaniola called Madanio: affirming it to be inhabited only with women: to whom the cannibals have access at certain times of the year, as in old time the Thracians had to the Amazons in the Island of Lesbos" (Arber 1885:69). Again, Martyr talks of the carved images the inhabitants make: "In these they grave the lovely Images of such fantasies as they suppose they see walk by night which the Antiquitie called Lemurs." And again in speaking of their Zemes, or spirits, Martyr says,

> These Zemes they believe to send plenty and fruitfulness of the roots, as the antiquitie believed such fairies or spirits as they called Dryades, Hamadryades, Satyros, Panes, and Nereides, to have the care and providence of the sea, woods, and springs and fountains, assigning to every peculiar thing their peculiar gods. Even so do the inhabitants of this island attribute a Zemes to everything supposing the same to give ear to their invocations. (Arber 1885:101)

Not only did knowledge of Ancient Greek customs provide a necessary resource in order to understand the practices of the inhabitants of the New World but a close scrutiny of the New Worlder's beliefs and customs turned out to shed great light on what the Ancient Greeks believed. Martyr recounts one of the "myths" of the inhabitants that relates how men once lived without women. In those days men dwelled in the damp darkness of a great cave. One day while coming out for one of their food gathering journeys, they

21

suddenly espy some women by a pond who appear to them as slippery as eels, and who are without "privie parts." The men hurriedly capture them, use a long beaked bird to make their vaginas, and henceforth are able to produce off-spring. After recounting this "myth" Martyr is suddenly overwhelmed with an insight:

> But now do I cease to marvel that the old Greeks did fable and write so many books on the people called Myrmidones, which they feigned to be engendered of ants of pissemeres. These and such like the sagest and wisest of the people preach continually to the simple sort, and rehearse the same as most holy oracles. But it is yet more childish that they fable as touching the original of the sea. (Arber 1885:100)

The peculiarness, and the otherness of the beliefs and practices of these New Worlders is of the same order as the peculiarness and otherness of the Ancient Greeks.[4] One illuminates the other.

Sahagun also establishes a series of equivalences between the Aztec and Roman gods: "The goddess they called Chicomecoatl. This is another Ceres." "The goddess of water, whom they called Chalchiuhtlicue; this is another Juno." "The goddess of carnal things, whom they called Tlazolteotl, another Venus," etc. As Todorov notes, this conceptual framework "keeps Sahagun from understanding, for example, the nature of the supreme divinity (one of whose names is Tezcatlipoca), since such a divinity is invisible and intangible, is its own origin, creator of history but itself without history; Sahagun *expects the Aztecs gods to resemble the Roman gods, not the God of the Christians!*" (Todorov 1984:233, emphasis mine). The initial strange uniqueness of the New Worlders' practices loses its utter strangeness and becomes more general, more common. These practices and beliefs became intelligible because they were seen in a relation of repetition, of analogical repetition, with the Ancient Greeks. And, reciprocally, the seemingly invincible strangeness of the Greeks finally became less alien, less imcomprehensible, insofar as it could be related to the practices and customs of the inhabitants of the New World. The alienness of the pre-Christian past became suddenly familiarized in simultaneity with the alienness of the extra-Christian present. In this strange dialectic of strangeness the strange and alien customs of the New World became less strange, became more comprehensible *in virtue of* a comparison, in virtue of the *act of comparison*, with the equally strange and alien customs of Greek Antiquity. Cosmography rests here on an analogy without familiarity, i.e., on an analogy neither of whose terms are familiar. The unknown was not explained by the known but was rather imaginatively brought into the vicinity of, and compared to, another unknown, which suddenly and on contact willy-nilly transformed both unknowns into knowns. The obscurely threatening velocity of the rediscovery of the Ancient World, the Ancient Greeks, was thereby disarmed and contained by *comparison with* the discovery of the New World, and, obversely, the discovery of the New World was confined by means of *a comparison* with the limited and short-circuited rediscovery of Antiquity.[5] The comparitist attitude and way of seeing is what is decisive:

> The comparatist puts certain *objects*, all of which are external to him, on the same level, and he himself remains the sole subject. The comparison, in Sahagun, as in Las Casas, affects the gods of *others*: of the Aztecs, of the Romans, of the Greeks; it does not put the Other on the same level as oneself, and does not call into question ones own categories. (Todorov 1984:240)

GOLD AND SPICES AND THE OTHER

"Your Highnesses have here another world in which our Holy Faith may be so propagated and whence may be taken so much wealth," writes Columbus; and Vasco da Gama, when questioned by an Eastern prince as to what it was he sought, replied, with all of Europe, "Christians and spices." How is that "and" possible? How is that conjunction, that coexistence of "Christians *and* spices," "Christians *and* gold," possible? It is perhaps a strange conjunction, like looking for apples and Eskimos or Volkswagons and quasars. What authorized the possibility of this historically specific juxtaposition? As Foucault says in *The Order of Things*, the *and* of enumeration has as a condition of its conceivability the *in* where the things enumerated would be divided up. What is the "*in*" in sixteenth-century cosmography? What is that common and containing intellectual space? What is that supporting volume?

What did the explorers have to *know* in order to do what they did? The explorers did not merely drift across the face of an as yet unformulated world, of a not-yet-discovered-world. They were not just randomly looking; they were looking *for*. Discovery was a project and a practice in the sixteenth century, unlike the Middle Ages. It was an essentially intentional undertaking, rather than an es-

23

sentially accidental happening. The explorers intended to discover, to find. They were looking for gold, for spices, for colonies, and commerce, and only in relation to this quest can their quest for "knowledge," for knowledge of other peoples and lands be understood.

The project of exploration, the era of exploration, was suffused with commercialism. Indeed, it was commercialism and its subsidiary, the commercially sponsored "desire for knowledge" that lay at the foundation of this enterprise and was integral to its very possibility. Exploration in the sixteenth century (the "Golden Age," the "Age of Gold") cannot be understood apart from commerce and commercial exploitation. Exploration as a "quest for knowledge" was almost entirely grounded upon exploration as commercial exploitation, and when it did produce revolutionizing knowledge, bursting the world of commercial concerns and interests—as it does most dramatically in the ontology of geography, where there occurs a tremendous change in the nature, structure, function and objects of geographical knowledge—it was not by design, by intention, by a positive quest for knowledge, but rather by accident, by new, curious, and finally disturbing circumstances ("anomalies" in Kuhn's sense) that spun off from the project of establishing the greatest possible system of commercial exploitation.

The non-European Other was seen then on the horizon of Renaissance commerce and was contained and imprisoned, essentially, within a commercial perception. He was taken into account, shaped, classified and deployed within the network of commercial concerns. The Other was seen laterally, as it were next to, along side of, and in front of, "gold and spices." As Las Casas says, "I do not say that they want to kill them [the Indians] directly, from the hate they bear them; they kill them because they want to be rich and have much gold, which is their whole aim . . . " (as quoted in Todorov 1984:142). The Other had a kind of derivative reality, a secondary and derivative visibility dependent upon the desired gold and spices: he was seen obscurely, next to the dazzling glitter of gold and amidst the exotic perfume of spices. In other respects he was invisible, as Sebastian Munster reported in his Universal Cosmography (1551).

Whereat as the Spainards marvelled, the men of the island told them, that not far from thence was another island in which were a kind of men not only with hanging ears, but also with

24

ears of such breadth and length, that with one of them they might cover their whole head. But the Spainards, who sought for gold and spices, and not for monsters, sailed directly to the island of Molucca. (Arber 1885:34)

Columbus also manifests this phenomenon:

> Gold—or rather the search for it . . . is omnipresent in the course of Columbus's first voyage. On the very day following the discovery, October 13, 1492, he already notes in his diary: "I was attentive and worked hard to know if there was any gold" and he returns to this subject unceasingly: "I do not wish to delay but to discover and go to many islands to find gold.". . . His very prayer has become "Our Lord in his goodness guide me that I may find this gold." (Todorov 1984:8)

In this cosmographical discourse of the sixteenth century there was a persistent, nay, a relentless preoccupation with formulating the nature of the relationship between the strangeness of the non-European Other and the gold he lives next to. This displays, in one direct sense, the need to justify the appropriation of this gold, but also, more obliquely, this displays the opportunity and the need to gain a self-understanding of the European's desire for this gold. Within this matrix of desire, gold, appropriation, responsibility, and differentiation, we may mark two primary formulations of the non-European Other—formulas that later were to be cut adrift from the original contexts and concerns that made them possible and generated them, and that would become, henceforth, susceptible to any meaning one chose to give them: The Other is inferior to the European because he is not, as the European is, capable of having a responsible relationship with this gold that surrounds him, and hence the European appropriation of it is justified. This formulation we may term the Other-as-Child. Fray Pedro de Feria, Bishop of Chiapa, submitted in 1585 a memorandum to the third Mexican Provincial Council wherein he states, "We must love and help the Indians as much as we can. But their base and imperfect character requires that they should be ruled, governed, and guided to their appointed end by fear more than by love. . . . These people do not know how to judge the gravity of their sins other than by the rigour of the penalties with which they are punished." After quoting the good Bishop, Elliott, in his *The Discovery of America and the Discovery of Man*, goes on to say, "In the bishop's words we hear the echoes of the sixteenth century schoolroom; and it was indeed as archetypal children that many of the Spainish religious, irrespective of their order, came to look upon the Indians" (Elliott 1972:13). In reference to gold and spices the non-European Other is a child, but an adult child, a man-child, i.e., he is not equal to his own desires. It is not that he is in fact not maintaining a responsible relationship to the objects that he and we desire, as a lazy and incompetent adult, but that he is in principle incapable of having a responsible relationship to them.

Or, secondly, the Other is superior to the European in that he is above the European's enslavement to his own greed and lust for gold; he does not desire what the European desires . . . and hence once again the European's appropriation of this gold is justified. This formulation we may term the Other-as-Saint. Not that he is now capable of being responsible to the objects of his desires, but now he has, in principle, no need of these objects; he has, in principle, no mundane, worldly desires.

The very possibility of experiencing the need to justify the appropriation of gold and spices (and land, and labor, and life, etc.) necessarily assumes that there *is* a relationship between the Other and gold. What are the constitutive conditions necessary for this type of relationship to be given to cosmography?

The relationship of the Renaissance to the Middle Ages and to antiquity has two sides and two meanings; and nowhere does this duality show itself more clearly than in the Renaissance position on the problem of self-consciousness. All the intellectual currents that nourish the Renaissance flow into this central problem. . . . The conscious formulation of these questions is, of course, one of the latest products of Renaissance philosophy, first attained by Descartes. . . . Descartes discovered and defined the new "Archimedian" point from which the conceptual world of scholastic philosophy could be raised out of its hinges. And thus we date the beginning of modern philosophy from Descartes' principle of the Cogito. . . . With one blow, with an independent, unique decision, the mind rejects the whole of the past and must now go along the new path towards thoughtful reflection upon itself. This is not a question of a gradual evolution but of a genuine "revolution in the mode of thought." And the significance of this revolution is by no means lessened if we trace the development and

26

the steady growth of the intellectual and the general forces
which finally gave it birth. At first, these forces do not con-
stitute a unity, nor do they show any rigid organization. . . .
Nevertheless, they all have one negative result in common: they
loosen up, so to speak, the earth out of which will come forth
the new, specifically modern view of the relationship of "subject" and "object." There is scarcely a single branch of Renaissance philosophy that did not participate in this task—not
only metaphysics but natural philosophy and empirical
knowledge of nature; not only psychology but ethics and aes-
thetics. (Cassirer 1963:123)

And, we can now add, cosmography. For Renaissance cosmography the non-European Other must be experienced as a Subject over
and against an Object, i.e., the Other must be circumscribed by,
and experienced within, a Subject-Object ontology. The Other is
simultaneously seen as, and denied as, a force of contestation, and
it is precisely here that he is seen as not-adult-but-child and as
adult-but-saint. Hence the possibility of affording war, of direct
competition, is both experienced and denied. The Other is encountered neither in the dangerous and perpetually unstable equilib-
rium of a subject-relation, nor is he fully and definitively contained
and circumferenced in the secure quiescence of an object-relation.

Things have changed little since Columbus who . . . also captured the Indians in order to complete a kind of naturalist's
collection, in which they took their place alongside plants and
animals . . . the Other was reduced to the status of an object.
Cortez does not have the same point of view, but the Indians
have still not become subjects in the full sense of the word,
i.e., subjects comparable to the *I* who contemplates and con-
ceives them. They occupy rather an intermediate status in his
mind: they are subjects certainly, but subjects reduced to the
role of producers of objects. (Todorov 1984:130)

Within the discursive universe of sixteenth-century cosmography, the non-European Other is experienced not directly as a Subject—retaining his sovereign violence and his violent sovereignty—nor directly as an Object—already stripped, silent,
speechless, devoid of all power and interest save that of being an
object of power and interest—but rather indirectly as a Subject
over and against an Object. His power of transcendence is thereby

27

both assumed and employed, and in that employment is frozen, fixed, and disarmed. From the perspective of cosmography and commerce he is seen, as it were, constantly in profile, never as full face. His eyes are diverted toward the commercial object, gold, spices, land, etc., in reference to which he is defined, and he is seen as seeing, and hence the possibility of exercising on us his power of transcendence, his power of interrogation,[6] is permanently side-tracked, permanently disarmed. Sixteenth-century cosmography deploys the Other in a space such that, like the animal in a zoo cage, he is perpetually and constantly available to our eyes, radically and permanently visible, entailing thereby the equally radical and permanent invisibility of the European: cosmography wishes to simultaneously preserve the possibility of seeing the Other while annihilating the anxiety of the possibility of being seen by the Other. Todorov comes to, I believe, a similar conclusion, though with a different emphasis:

> Columbus's attitude with regard to the Indians is based on his perception of them. We can distinguish here two component parts which we shall find . . . in practice, down to our own day. . . . Either he conceives the Indians . . . as human beings altogether, having the same rights as himself; but then he sees them not only as equals but also as identical, and this behavior leads to assimilationism, the projection of his own values on the other. Or else he starts from the difference, but the latter is immediately translated into terms of superiority and inferiority. . . . What is denied is the existence of a human substance truly other, something capable of being not merely an imperfect state of oneself. These two elementary figures of the experience of alterity are both grounded in egocentrism, in the identification of our own values with values in general, of our *I* with the universe—in the conviction that the world is one. (Todorov 1984:42)

COPERNICUS AND COLUMBUS: THE TRANSFORMATION OF SPACE

In his sixteenth-century *Treatise of the Sphere* Pedro Nunes succinctly formulated his problem and his anxiety as a cosmographer, "New islands, new lands, new seas, new peoples; and, what is more, a new sky and new stars." The sixteenth century underwent two obscurely linked and profoundly altering "paradigm revolutions": one in "astronomy" and the other in "geography." We associate Copernicus' name with the paradigm revolution in astronomy, and, in the same way, we may mark the equally total transformation in the field of geography with the name of Columbus. Copernicus altered the astronomical imagination, the astronomical field, as Columbus altered the geographical imagination; and as Copernicus remained "conservative" (Copernicus 1947),[7] still profoundly Ptolemaic, having no idea of or commitment to an "infinite universe"—though laying the foundation for making possible such a concern and commitment—so Columbus, too, remained "conservative" (Columbus 1957, 1930), believing he had reached India, the East, as he had intended. The explorers and discoverers following upon Columbus profoundly altered geographical discourse, the science and imagination of geography, just as the astronomers and mechanics following upon Copernicus profoundly altered astronomical discourse. The "discovery" of the "New World" represents a paradigm revolution in geographical discourse as the "discovery" of "heliocentrism" represents a paradigm revolution in astronomical discourse.

A self-conscious formulation of the rupture in the geographical tradition experienced in sixteenth-century cosmography would sound something like, "It is a striking fact that our classical authors had no knowledge of all this America, which we call new lands." So wrote the Parisian lawyer Etienne Pasquir in the early 1560s. If the ancients were wrong in some of the places on the maps they have left us, they could be wrong in many other, and perhaps all, places. The maps of the world handed down to us by the ancients are wrong—and we have proved this not by new maps, but by experience. For sixteenth-century cosmography the entire project of the discovery and exploration of the world was, in one decisive sense, experienced as a direct refutation of the ancients—both Medieval and pagan—and hence as a direct refutation of the authority of their "map of the world," of their cosmography. Sixteenth-century cosmography partakes then of that more general Renaissance shift in the experience of authority to the authority of experience. As Leonardo said in reply to the Scholastics, "If I cannot cite authors, as you can, I shall nonetheless cite a much greater and worthier thing, in that I refer myself to experience, the master of your masters."

Only in the "Age of Exploration" did a "map" become an *in-*

strument to *practically use* rather than, as previously, a symbol to read, decipher, and meditate upon. Medieval maps of the world

> were not so much aids to travel, or to the imagining of actual relationship of one land mass to another, but visual commemorations of divine purpose, commonly with Jerusalem at the center and the rest of creation grouped about it. . . . Medieval maps were more for reflection or delight than use. They were symbols of God's power, repositories of legends and marvels, the visual equivalents of Genesis. Even when the influence of ancient geography gained ground, the maps that reflected it were tributes to the newly discovered classical authorities rather than things to use. (Hale 1967:336)

Somewhat after the early explorations of Prince Henry the Navigator, and totally after Columbus' voyages, geographical discourse became for the first time a practical matter of experience concerned with measuring and describing (Van Helden 1985). It collapsed, as it were, into the one-dimensional plane of the nomination of the visible—with the overtones that "naming" has in the sixteenth century: a matter of transcribing the visible world, rather than, as hitherto, speculating on and deciphering the nature, form, and strucure of the world (using the ancient resources of symmetry, derived principally from Herodotus, and analogy, and legend). Also the possibility of citing the Bible as support for geographical statements, hitherto an operative form in geography (a distant relative perhaps to our contemporary operative form of "citing facts"), was alienated from geographical discourse.

GEOGRAPHICAL AND ASTRONOMICAL DISCOVERY

Referring to the sixteenth century, Michelet wrote in a famous passage, "Two things belong to this age more than to all its predecessors: the discovery of the world, and the discovery of man." Discovery is not so much the concreete *seeing of a new thing* as it is rather a *new way of seeing things*. Contrary to the positivistic historical tradition, the meaning of Columbus' voyage was not that of verifying a hypothesis—as for instance in Samuel Morison's *Admiral of the Ocean Sea, A Life of Christopher Columbus* (1943). Only under the optical illusion of retrospective historizing can it be said that Columbus "discovered America" (O'Gorman 1961). Columbus, rather, initiated the paradigm revolution in geography and cosmography whereby "America" *and also the world that could contain such an entity* were slowly constructed. Columbus' "discovery of America" does not represent the finding of some new thing, "America," that was always silently there (merely hitherto unknown), but rather a profound paradigm revolution in the science and practice of geography and the geographical imagination. If we can abandon the security, if we can subvert the positivistic notion that Copernicus "discovered" heliocentrism, and that, one sunny day in 1492, Columbus "discovered" America, we can, I believe, greatly benefit the historical understanding of the development of scientific discourse. The positivist formulation of discovery invariably collapses and impoverishes the concept of "discovery" wholly into an externality, into the neutralized recognition of an externality. Neither Columbus' "America" nor Copernicus' "heliocentrism" was, however, a factual discovery within an existing framework of ideas, but rather the radical and constitutive invention of a new and different framework. An elucidating example is given by Peter Winch, in his *The Idea of a Social Science*.

> In speaking of "new ideas" I shall make a distinction. Imagine a biochemist making certain observations and experiments as a result of which he discovers a new germ which is responsible for a certain disease. In one sense we might say that the name he gives to this new germ expresses a new idea, but I prefer to say in this context that he has made a discovery within an existing framework of ideas. I am assuming that the germ theory of disease is already well established in the scientific language he speaks. Now compare with this discovery the impact made by the first formulation of that theory, the first introduction of the concept of germ into the language of medicine [of "heliocentrism" into the language of astronomy, of "America" into the language of geography]. This was a much more radically new departure, involving not merely a new factual discovery within an existing way of looking at things, but a completely new way of looking at the whole problem of the causation of diseases. . . . (Winch 1958:121)

In the *Invention of America* Edmundo O'Gorman, a Spanish historian who has been influenced by Heidegger and who is in close proximity to Winch's position, sees the gradual emergence of "America" on the sixteenth-century horizon of European concern not as an instantaneous act of "discovery" but rather as a slow, constructive, historical process of "invention."

> "Discovery" implies that the nature of the thing found was previously known to the finder, i.e., that he knows that objects such as the one he has found can and do exist, although the existence of that particular one was wholly unknown. Thus an astronomer who is already aware that some heavenly bodies are classed as planets may be said to have "discovered" a planet when he detects for the first time one of those bodies. But the astronomer who first has the conception of such bodies as "planets" may properly be said to have "invented" that class of heavenly bodies, since it was he who formulated for the first time the concept itself. (O'Gorman 1961:9)

In the sixteenth century it is principally the geographical imagination in deep linkage with the astronomical imagination that performs the philosophical function of furnishing a site on and in which to live, that is preoccupied with the concern "Where are we?" The geographical and astronomical revolution mark the profound invention of a new place, a new space in which "man" may live. The slow infinitization and homogenization of astronomical space in the sixteenth century proceeds, it would seem, in strict analogy with the slow expansion and homogenization of geographical space.

In the geography of the fifteenth century there were no "continents" and there were no "oceans" (Cassidy 1968). The world in the fifteenth century was geographically pictured as an Island. It was experienced as being something essentially insular, surrounded by the dark, inhuman and unknowable void of the deep waters. The gradual appearance and construction of what is now called "America" on the horizon of European history in the sixteenth century was to change all that. The fifteenth-century world-space, derived mostly from rather degenerated versions of Ptolemy's geography, consisted of a relatively small, symmetrical pattern of Europe, Asia, and Africa with the Holy City of Jerusalem in the center and the night of the Ocean all around (Beazley 1949, 3:500 and Hale 1967:318). The world was, specifically and exactly, the *Orbis Terrarum*, the Island of the Earth:

From very ancient times up to recent years, it has been held that, in this life, the world is exclusively confined to the earth. Since the human body was thought of as being in essence nothing but earth, earth was its proper element and, therefore, the cosmic body where this element was predominant (or, to be more exact, that portion of it not submerged under the Ocean) was considered the "natural place" for human life. In ancient classical times the world was conceived as contained entirely within the Orbis Terrarum, i.e., the Island of the Earth. (O'Gorman 1961:66)

There was no "ocean" in the fifteenth century in our modern sense—the "oceans" mode of being was very different. The Ocean of the fifteenth century functioned as the parameter, as the *limit of the world*:

Ptolemy by himself was a warning against rather than an argument for an attempt to reach Cathay by circumnavigating Africa. . . . Nor did he suggest that the "Ocean Sea"—the deep waters outside normal fishing and coastal voyages which were believed to be different from them in kind—provided a medium in which men could survive. To the Middle Ages the Ocean Sea was rather like the upper atmosphere before the invention of oxygen masks and pressurized aircraft, a fatal zone delineating the physical limits of existence. (Hale 1967:336)

It is not that the Ocean was as yet empirically unknown, but rather that it was, in principle, unknowable.

The world was conceived as lodged on the earth and nowhere else, because, that being man's element, the earth was the "natural place" for his world. The unavoidable conclusion was that the rest of the universe is something foreign and alien to man, something that at no time and under no circumstances could become part of this world. . . . This important conclusion is illustrated in the role played by the Ocean in this period of history. The Ocean was a tangible instance of the indifference and strangeness of cosmic reality, because although it combines with earth to make up the globe that man inhabits, it also constitutes the limits of his world; from the geographical point of view, the Ocean was nothingness or void, it was not considered susceptible of juridical possession or of being an object on which the sovereignty of princes could be exercised. (O'Gorman 1961:67)

With Columbus' voyages and the multiple chains of events they initiated, a great disquiet appears on the horizon of Renaissance Europe; a disquiet in profound propinquity to the great transformations we mark with the Copernican Revolution. Within cosmographical discourse after Columbus the Orbis Terrarum, the Island of the Earth, undergoes a change in status analogically equivalent in its radicalness and depth to the change in status undergone by the "planet" earth in Copernican and post-Copernican astronomical discourse. Perhaps the most important document manifesting this world transformation is the *Cosmographiae Introduction*, published in 1507 by the Academy of St. Die, which includes, among other things, a Latin translation of Vespucci's *Letters* and a copy of Waldseemuller's engraved world map of 1507. It is in the language of this document that we may see expressed for the first time the hitherto nonexistent geographical category of "continents" and the hitherto nonexistent geographical object, the ocean:

It will be remembered that according to the traditional concept, the Orbis Terrarum was bounded by the Ocean and any other land that might exist was not, by definition, a part of the Orbis. But now, since the newly found lands, despite their insular character, are conceived as part of the Orbis Terrarum in the *Cosmographie Introduction* we can only conclude that in the new way of understanding it the Ocean is no longer regarded as its boundary. The ancient idea of the Orbis Terrarum as man's world is now for the first time conceived as including not only the Island of the Earth, but the Ocean itself, and therefore, not only the new found lands but any other land that may appear in the future; the Orbis Terrarum is thus identified with the entire terraqueous globe. (O'Gorman 1961:128)

With this radical change in the nature and extent, the quality and quantity, of geographical space, the old organizing schema of the Orbis Terrarum bounded by the impenetrably dark ocean gives way to the schema of the "earth's surface" and to the geographical classification and organization of the earth's surface in terms of "con-

THE OTHER IN THE RENAISSANCE

tinents" and "oceans." The insularity of the world, the Orbis Terrarum, is burst when the ocean looses its historically unique being
and undergoes the profound mutation from being an indefinite limit
to being a circumscribed object.

> We must first ask ourselves why America was placed on an
> equal footing not, as might be expected, with the Orbis Ter-
> rarum as a whole, but with the three individual parts that made
> up that whole. This question is easily answered if we bear in
> mind that in the new picture of the world the ocean has been
> included. The ocean therefore ceased to play its ancient role
> of defining the boundaries of the World. The discontinuity of
> two land masses imposed by an intervening ocean became a
> mere geographical accident; the ocean as a boundary became
> no more significant than a river or a mountain range which
> forms the boundary between two provinces without inter-
> rupting the continuity of the land that contains them. Hence
> the idea of placing America on an equal footing with Europe,
> Asia, and Africa and not with the old Orbis Terrarum as a whole
> was not only possible but inevitable. . . . If the land surface
> of the globe is considered as a continuous whole, it follows
> that Europe, Asia, Africa, and America are contiguous lands.
> Thus we finally reach the concept under which these four en-
> tities were considered similar, namely, the concept of "con-
> tinental" lands, since, in its primary sense, "continental" means
> "contiguous." (O'Gorman 1961:131)

ASTRONOMY AND COSMOGRAPHY AS CRITIQUE

The two spaces opened up by the paradigm revolution of Copernican astronomy and the paradigm revolution of post-Columbian
cosmography provided for the production of analogically related
new problems, new questions, and new anxieties. The linkage of
these two spaces accounts for the similarity in the anxiety simultaneously experienced within both disciplines in regard to their
relationship with the larger surrounding constellation of discourses and in regard to their relationship to the larger context of
Christian life, i.e., with their relationship to the metaphysical and
moral commitment to the Christian cosmology and the Christian
drama of life.

The "explorer" of the sixteenth century was, unlike the earlier Medieval travelers, of necessity also a "critic":

> Marco Polo and other Medieval travelers of whom we have knowledge were as curious about what they saw as were their Renaissance successors, and they were hardly more credulous. But their curiosity was more indiscriminate and taking their world picture for granted, they neither criticized it nor felt the need to relate their experiences to it. . . . The Renaissance explorer on the other hand was not only opening up new territory and new routes, he was constantly adjusting his inheritance of guesses about what the world looked like in the light of what he found. (Hale 1967:334)

In the sixteenth century, for the first time, *exploration* becomes possible. The sixteenth-century explorer, the geographical explorer, functioned as the perpetual resident critic of the sixteenth-century world-picture, just as the sixteenth- and seventeenth-century astronomer, astronomical explorer, did. Later Galileo will become perhaps the most outstanding embodiment of astronomy as critique and of astronomical discourse as having the organizational function of critical consciousness. The cosmography of the sixteenth and seventeenth centuries is brought into proximity with the astronomy of the late sixteenth and seventeenth centuries in that both assumed a unique and historically specific critical function in relation to the contemporaneous moral, philosophical, and religious discourses that surrounded them. It was not merely an arbitrary, accidental, and external affair for sixteenth- and seventeenth-century geographical and astronomical discourses that they happened to be uncompromisingly, crucially, and terminally critical of many of their sixteenth- and seventeenth-century neighboring discourses, of their discursive environment, and especially of theological cosmology. It was rather constitutive of their very formation. In this one can perhaps see a parallel with nineteenth-century "geology" and "evolutionary biology" and their relationships to their neighboring discourses.

For both astronomy and cosmography the decisive altering and critical function took place around the experience of an essential centrality, of astronomical centrality, of geographical centrality (perhaps, of human centrality), and both were obscurely linked by means of a geometry of values to moral centrality, to the centrality of morals: of being the significant point, equidistant from all other points on the periphery. Both cosmography and astronomy became, in their own ways, critical modes for the assertion of an essential peripheralness. As Giordano Bruno had earlier proclaimed in his heretical *On The Infinite Universe and Worlds*, "There is in the universe neither centre nor circumference, but if you will, the whole is central, and every point may be regarded as part of a circumference to some other central point." The road traveled was that of a geocentric to a heliocentric to an anticentric—a centerless, pointless—view of both the universe about the earth and the lands and peoples dispersed over the surface of the earth.

THE FACES OF THE OTHER

In post-Copernican astronomy the theological heavens are transformed into an astronomical space. In post-Columbian cosmography the dark, opaque, impenetrable Ocean together with the secure, privileged, Jerusalem-centered Orbis Terrarum are transformed into a geographical space. Both the new space of astronomy and the new space of geography inexorably, unrelentingly, and weightily bear down upon that tenuous figure, "Christian man." They bear down upon the anxiety of his place and, above all, upon his identity *in reference to the Other* whom he now must encounter and account for; for at the foundations of both the new astronomy and the new cosmography there is the cosmological axiom that space is essentially inhabitable space, that the newly "discovered" space is essentially anthropomorphic space, and that for any given piece of space there will be, of necessity, new beings that inhabit that space. In speaking of the Copernican Revolution, Kuhn says,

> More than a picture of the universe and more than a few lines of Scripture were at stake. The drama of Christian life and the morality that had been made dependent upon it would not readily adopt to a universe in which the earth was just one of a number of planets [or Europe just one of a number of continents]. . . . When it was taken seriously, Copernicus' proposal [as that of post-Columbian cosmography] raised many gigantic problems for the believing Christian. If, for example, the earth were merely one of six planets [as now the former

Island of the Earth is merely a close group of continents among other continents], how were the stories of the Fall and of the Salvation, with their immense bearing on Christian life, to be preserved? If there were other bodies essentially like the earth [other continents essentially like Europe], God's goodness would surely necessitate that they, too, be inhabited. But if there were men on other planets [and if there were men on other continents, in the "Americas"] how could they be descendents of Adam and Eve, and how could they have inherited original sin, which explains man's otherwise incomprehensible travail on an earth made for him by a good and omnipotent deity? Again, how could men on other planets [in the Americas] know of the Savior who opened to them the possibility of eternal life? (Kuhn 1957:193)

The foundation upon which and the concerns in relation to which a kind of "science fiction" in the sixteenth and seventeenth centuries would rest, stand, it would seem, in a complementary and analogous relation to the foundations and concerns of a contemporaneous "anthropology." The Other is encountered as it were from within the same perspective. The possible problems of the mode of being of the Other, of his relation with man and God and of man's relation to him, were located on the same horizon for both the "anthropology" of the sixteenth and seventeenth centuries and for that segment and concern of astronomical discourse that we could call "science fiction" or "celestial anthropology." The possible beings that could be encountered on earth and in the heavens were the same; the terrestrial Other and the celestial Other were, of necessity, of the same order.

The historical way of seeing embedded in the remarks of a contemporary astronomer toward his ancestors are revealing in this context (especially those points seen as "curious knowledge" and their repercussions toward the soundness or foolishness of "our knowledge"):

Huygens (1629–1695) was, to be sure, not a thoroughly modern astronomer; he could not entirely escape the modes of belief of his time. Consider the curious argument by which he deduced the existence on Jupiter of hemp. Galileo had observed four moons traveling around Jupiter. Huygens asked a question of a kind few astronomers would ask today: Why is

38

it that Jupiter has four moons? Well, why does the earth have one moon? Our moon's function, Huygens reasoned, apart from providing a little light at night and raising the tides, is to aid mariners in navigation. If Jupiter has four moons, there must be many mariners on that planet. Mariners imply boats, boats imply sails, sails imply ropes. And ropes imply hemp. I sometimes wonder how many of our own prized scientific arguments will appear equally foolish from the vantage of three centuries. (Sagan 1975:25)

For a relatively long time after the mutation of the Ptolemaic cosmos into the Copernican cosmos it was—within that constituted imaginative-epistemological network that lasted intact from the early sixteenth through the eighteenth century—directly and immediately conceivable, indeed, it was almost a necessity that "men lived on other planets." It wasn't until the nineteenth-century reorganization of knowledge that there took place a juncture between astronomical discourse and that discourse which originated the condition of the conceivability of "life," of the "conditions of life," and of the "organism-and-environment," i.e., evolutionary biological discourse; it wasn't until then that the possibility of "men on other planets" ceased being a serious possibility of discourse and began being, from the positive perspective of Darwinian astronomy, an ironic fable attributable to the "curious ignorance" of "earlier," "less scientific" ages. It would appear an almost intransient characteristic of the positivist perspective that it *accounts for difference* in knowledge, in practices, in beliefs, by *denying difference* via such resources as "ignorance," "earlier," and "less scientific," i.e., its account of difference does not *preserve* the difference it accounts for but rather destroys that difference. It accounts for difference by transforming difference into ignorance that thereby destroys its original character as difference.

THE HOMOGENIZATION OF SPACE

Within the Medieval cosmos heirarchy (the ecclesiastical principle) was the omnipresent principle not only of ordering and specifying value but also of determining essence itself. The objects located in the immutable astronomical-theological heavens, as those located on the corruptible earth, assumed their nature from their place.

39

The place they occupied was internal to them; it held an intrinsic, immanent, formative influence upon their being. The ordering, living heterogeneity of astronomical and cosmographical space determined in advance and with sufficiency the kind of face the objccts found there would present to the astronomer and cosmographer. For the Aristolelean-Medieval cosmology:

> Places have their nature and peculiar characteristics, the same as bodies—or, if not the same, at least in an analogous way. . . . The body is by no means indifferent to the place in which it is located and by which it is enclosed; rather it stands in a real and causal relation to it. Every physical element seeks 'its' place, the place that belongs and corresponds to it, and flees from any other opposed to it. (Cassirer 1963:175)

After Copernicus and after Columbus this epistemic framework that provided for what is experienced and recognized as self-evident changed and henceforth the general relationship of any object to the place in which it is located became essentially a relationship of indifferent exteriority.

> One of the most important tasks of Renaissance philosophy and mathematics [and geography] was the creation, step by step, of the conditions for a new concept of space. The task ws to replace *aggregrate space* by *system space*, i.e., to replace space as a *substratum* by space as a *function*. Space had to be stripped of its objectivity, of its substantial nature, and had to be discovered as a free, ideal complex of lines. The first step on this path consisted in establishing the general principle of the homogeneity of space. (Cassirer 1963:182)

> Astronomical and cosmographical space became, for the first time, self-evidently uniforn and homogenous. With this the theoretical and practical geographical project of representationally and symbolically covering the earth's surface with homogenous lines of longitude and latitude in complete indifference to the specific nature of the areas covered was made possible. At the heart of both the new astronomy and the new cosmography lay both the presupposition and the project, however remote its final realization, of the homogenization of space. This becomes selfconsciously manifested in Descartes.

> The old opposition of the earthly world of change and decay to the changeless world of the skies which, as we have seen,

was not abolished by the Copernican revolution, but persisted as the opposition of the moving world of the sun and the planets to the motionless fixed stars, disappears without trace. The unification and uniformization of the universe in its contents and laws becomes a self-evident fact: "The matter of the sky and the earth is one and the same; and there cannot be a plurality of worlds." (Koyre 1957:105)

This predetermines and fixes in advance the nature and kind of Other that can and will be encountered. This gives the Other his a priori.

In post-Copernican astronomy, the earth becomes *a planet*, just as, after Columbus, Europe becomes *a continent*. When Europe becomes a "continent" there will be numerous "Europes" and therefore numerous non-European Others who are very different yet somehow the same. When the earth becomes a "planet" there will be six "earths" and numerous extraterrestrial earthlings. When the earth is thrust into the heavens the heavens collapse into the earth. "If the earth is a celestial body it must show the immutability of the heavens and the heavens in turn must participate in the corruption of the earth" (Kuhn 1957:105).

Because of the absolute interpenetration of "astrology" and "astronomy" in the Renaissance, the same movement toward reciprocity is experienced in "astrology."

This emanantistic sort of physics presented by Ficino is still completely in accord with the old presentations, especially with the *Picatrix*, the classical handbook of late Hellenistic magic and astrology. But it cannot be sustained much longer for its most solid foundation was destroyed when the philosophical thought of the Quattrocento completed its decisive criticism of the concept of the graduated cosmos. In the new cosmology, which begins with Nicholas Cusanus, there is not absolute "above" or "below," and, therefore, there can no longer be just one direction of influence. The idea of the world organism is here expanded in such a way that every element in the world may with equal right be considered the central point of the universe. The hitherto one-sided relationship of dependence between the lower and higher world now takes on more and more the form of a relationship of pure *correlation*. And therewith, the type and the foundation of astrological thought must gradually be transformed even where the general presuppo-

41

sitions of astrology remain in force. In Germany this transformation takes place most clearly in the philosophy of nature
of Paracelsus. (Cassirer 1963:182)

What Copernicus initiated in revising, in altering, and, in some
instances, collapsing the distance, the difference, and the otherness
between the earth and the heavens, between the terrestrial and the
celestial, Descartes and Newton, by way of Galileo and Kepler
brought to full fruition. With Newton, with absolute Newtonian
space, we may mark the radical and complete homogenization of
the universe, the complete physical as well as moral and symbolical uniformization of the cosmos. On a broad, global basis, it was
not until Descartes' and Newton's paradigmatic solidification of
astronomical discourse that "the heavens," the celestial, were considered as essentially uniform with, and governed by the same laws
as, the "earth," the terrestrial. The heavens become contiguous with
the earth just as Europe becomes contiguous with (i.e., becomes a
continent with) the other areas of the earth. Henceforth "Terrestrial experiments [for example the pendulum, the projectile] yield
direct knowledge of the heavens, and celestial observations give
information immediately applicable on earth" (Kuhn 1957:252). In
the same way as the heavens, the earth's surface too is conquered
by the Same. With the homogenization and uniformization of geographical space the Ocean Sea loses its unique being and becomes
no longer limit to, but object in the world; as the terrestrial–celestial difference so also the terrestrial–aquatic difference is ho-
mogenized.

II

THE OTHER
IN THE ENLIGHTENMENT

Thinking only begins at the point where we have come to know that Reason, glorified for centuries, is the most obstinate adversary of thinking.

Martin Heidegger

Frazer's presentation of the magical and religious views of men is unsatisfactory. . . . It makes these views appear as *errors*.

Ludwig Wittgenstein

ROBINSON CRUSOE AND THE OTHER

Defoe's *Robinson Crusoe* (1718) is a Bildungsroman at the heart of the early Enlightenment. It represents a belief in the odyssey as the method, par excellence, of acquiring both worldly wisdom (and gain, which is a part of that wisdom) and Christian knowledge. It brings about worldly wisdom by making true value visible and recognizable: "Thus we never see the true state of our condition till it is illustrated to us by its contraries; nor know how to value what we enjoy but by the want of it" (Rousseau)—or, as Carlyle was later to put it, "The healthy know not of their health, but only the sick." It is through the odyssey that we learn how absence makes true value present, how absence makes present the value of the absent. (Rousseau, later in the eighteenth century, considered *Robinson Crusoe* "The only book that teaches all that books can teach"; and, with a slight twist, by turning it inward as it were, in *Emile*, Rousseau employs and extends this methodology of absence in order to attain the truth of value, true value: "The surest way to raise oneself above prejudice, and order one's judgment on the real relationship between things, is to put oneself in the place of an isolated man, and to judge of everything as that man would judge of them, according to their actual usefulness" (Rousseau 1964:161).

43

The odyssey is a kind of eighteenth-century counterpart to the approach that will become solidified in the nineteenth century's "Comparative Method." The method of comparison makes value present, brings about the visibility of true value. The odyssey of Robinson Crusoe also brings about, produces, a Christian knowledge; it reveals God's plan and the obscure yet final justice of His government, the divine economy. It is an odyssey that bears constant witness to a theodicy.

Robinson Crusoe is Cartesian in his concrete, solipsistic solitude and his "desert island"; his outer isolation is a mirror to his "inner isolation." After almost eighteen years alone on his island during one of his walks Crusoe suddenly comes across the shore spread with human bones. It falls upon him violently like an unexpected blow: cannibals! He reels with sickness at the sight of the charred flesh, the picked skull, hand and leg bones. From the depths of his European body and soul he vomits. Later, after recovery and recomposure, Crusoe expends much thought upon "the savages"; prior to this calm, however, in the initial, raw encounter with this Otherness, Crusoe experiences what we might call the sovereignty of evil. The Christian experience of otherness within the framework of demonology is still operative here. He gazes directly into the eyes of the Other, into the abyss; for a fleeting moment he appears as one confronted with the autonomy of the diabolical, the flashing, gaping contradiction of the monstrous. The "savages" almost lose their distinctness on the indistinguishable background of hell:

> I was so astonished with the sight of these things that I entertained no notions of any danger to myself from it for a long while; all my apprehensions were buried in the thoughts of such a pitch of inhuman, hellish brutality, and the horror and degeneracy of human nature; which, though I had heard of often, yet I never had so near of a view of before; in short, I turned away my face from the horrid spectacle . . . for the aversion which nature gave me to these hellish wretches was such that I was fearful of seeing them as of seeing the Devil himself. . . . (Defoe 1961:163)

Crusoe, in the initial, unexpected, and violent experience of division, apprehends the savages as emblems of the infernal, as figures beyond "nature," figures manifesting the iconography of hell. No comparisons can yet be made in the midst of this whirl and

the penetration by
the "savage"

eddy of tumultuous movement. Crusoe, for a moment, is no longer
European master of his island, his miniature Europe. For a moment, as it were, the European is no longer master of Europe, of
his Europeanness, no longer master of his ideas, no longer master
of his mind. It is, as it were, a raw experience of the Other prior
to the moment when philosophical reflection comes to our aid. It
marks the eruption of the Other: an experience of the Other without the sedative of European philosophical interpretation. For a
moment the Other is beyond interpretation. If Crusoe could at this
moment have painted the "savages" they would surely appear more
as the infernal apparitions of Grunewald and Bosch than as the
"human" images of Rubens' or any of the Baroque's exotic non-
Europeans, or as Lafitau's American Indians. The realism of Man-
ichaeism, of the contradiction of evil, is pronounced and decisive
in Crusoe's first surge of thought. The evil of these savages is not
yet, as it was soon to become, an error, a pathology, the cause of
which lies in our inability to see the overall plan of God's design.
It is not due to an otherness of custom seen on the horizon of the
sovereignty of nations and national mores—as Crusoe would later
categorize and make sense of it. The reality of their evil is not re-
ducible, is not yet experienced as being-reducible-to-an-ultimately-
good-cause-that-is-not-revealed-to-human-thought. In the initial
violence of confrontation Crusoe's savages are irreducible; not a
flaw in the rationality of Providence but a contradiction to the rationality of Providence.

But soon, calm is restored, theodicy is reaffirmed and elaborated
upon, and the division is established. Instead of gazing at the Other
whose incomprehensible otherness is still intact and present, Crusoe subsumes this relation under a totalization that empowers him
to contain both the other and the self as units confronting one another in a neutralized totality (Levinas 1969). Crusoe rapidly re-
treats from the angle of direct confrontation in favor of, and in an
attempt to establish, the primacy of the panoramic. After first passionately planning to slaughter all the savages he could, he soon
has second thoughts:

> I began with cooler and calmer thoughts to consider what it
> was I was going to engage in: What authority or call I had to
> pretend to be judge and executioner upon these men as crim-
> inals, whom Heaven had thought fit for so many ages to suffer

unpunished to go on, and to be, as it were, the executioners of His judgements one upon another. How far these people were offenders against me, and what right I had to engage in the quarrel of that blood, which they promiscuously shed one upon another, I debated this very often with myself thus. How do I know what God Himself judges in this particular case? It is certain these people do not commit this as a crime; it is not against their own consciences' reproving, or their light reproaching them. They do not know it to be an offence, and then commit it in defiance of Divine justice, as we do in almost all the sins we commit. They think it no more a crime to kill a captive taken in war than we do to kill an ox; nor to eat human flesh, then we do to eat mutton. (Defoe 1961:168)

We are to some extent witnessing here the initial trajectory of Enlightenment and the initial trajectory of the Other: the Enlightenment's version of enlightenment and the "problem" of the Other is taking embryonic shape: the obscure intentions of God's design, the nature of his most singular government, collect here about the figure of the "savage." After Crusoe, the "savage" becomes the perpetual occasion to raise the question of the diversity of faiths, of ways of life, *in relation to God's design*, in relation to *theodicy*. First difference is, in a denial of and a rupture with the demonic, consciously humanized. It is intended, seen and affirmed *as human difference*, and simultaneously that human difference is experienced on the horizon of a Christian moral theodicy. It is to Christianity that the burden of explanation is deferred. A day would come in the nineteenth century when "God's design" would drop away and the diversity of these other ways of life would be understood "scientifically" in relation to the history and progress, or evolution, of civilization, to a different kind of theodicy. As Feuerbach's work would blaze forth to formulate it, the burden of explanation would be transferred from Christianity (God's design) to Anthropology.

Besides the Manichaean metaphysics of absolute otherness in respect of evil, and the Protestant ontology of relative deviance and difference in respect to God's design (the totality), Robinson Crusoe manifests a third method of ordering and experiencing the "savage": let us call it the instrumentalization of otherness. With the tremendous upheaval of the Scientific Revolution and the Reformation a new project, distinct from the Renaissance, becomes

46

possible for the West: man against nature. Man against nature as
a historical project, as an epistemological project, and as a practical, technical project. Unnatural man against un-human nature.
A vivid illustration of the essential "newness" and "difference" of
this project can perhaps be glimpsed in the difference and distance
between Sir Thomas More's *Utopia* (1516) and Francis Bacon's *New
Atlantis* (1624).

> More's values and concerns are all in terms of the establish-
> ment of God's "law of nature" among men—all in terms of
> the development of reason and true virtue in the individual,
> justice and tolerance in the state. His yardstick is the cardinal
> virtues of antiquity. But Bacon's vision is one of the harness-
> ing of the physical universe to the end of securing and ex-
> tending man's intellectual and physical well-being. *His* hu-
> manism is not of the classical variety, not immediately
> concerned with ideal values and the inner man, but rather with
> the improvement of human living conditions. . . . (Hayden
> 1961:18)

Robinson Crusoe upon first being cast on this solitary island feels
he must secure himself against wild beasts, savages, and the elements. "I consulted several things in my situation, which I found
would be proper for me: first, health and fresh water . . . secondly,
shelter from the heat of the sun; thirdly security from ravenous
creatures, whether man or beast . . ." (Defoe 1961:61). For the major part of his narrative Crusoe sees the "savage" through this project of "man against nature." The savage is seen on the background
of "nature" in "man against nature," and this a priori instrumentalization of "nature" has its counterpart in relation to the "savage." The duality of "European and savage" is ordered upon the
duality of "man against nature." In this respect, in the space of
classification, the "savage" is situated closer to the instrumental
elements of nature than he is to the moral valuations of action.
Crusoe's savages are seen on the surface of nature, i.e., that essentially homogenous space of resistance and danger, of recalcitrant
matter and threatening predators that must be instrumentally
overcome via techniques and technologies, that must be domesticated, ordered, humanized. For Crusoe, in this guise, the "savage"
is not a specifically human threat apart from nature but rather,
precisely, a threat of nature.

Crusoe meets many non–Europeans in his adventures. He is captured off the Guinia coast and made a house-slave by the Moors; on his plantation in Brazil he traffics with natives and wins a few African slaves; and finally, he meets, on his desert island, "Friday." "Friday," himself a cannibal, is saved by Crusoe from being devoured by other cannibals. Crusoe wishes to save him so that he may somehow use him to get off this desert island after more than twenty years. What is the very first thing—richly symbolical—that Crusoe, the eighteenth-century European, does with this cannibal, this "savage" whose life he has saved? He exercises the divine and sovereign right of christening: he names him. He proclaims that his name will be "Friday" and he will address Crusoe as "master." "Friday," in this reading, represents the entrance of the Other into the early eighteenth century, into Crusoe's world, into the world of the European Enlightenment. He represents the precarious metamorphosis of the limit of the Enlightenment *episteme* into an object for the Enlightenment *episteme* (a kind of epistemological imperialism). The cannibals had been in many respects the otherness of the world; they existed as a parameter, a limit to Crusoe's world, beyond his comprehension and beyond the threshold of his order. "Friday" undergoes the necessary transformation and becomes the other *in* Crusoe's world. He takes his assigned place as a subject inside that world, subject to, subjected to, its order. The Other is transformed into a subject of discourse and interaction by submitting his alienness for identification and domestication. Prior to being *named* he does not exist, he has no name of his own, no world of his own that would be intelligible to us. Similarly he has no language; Crusoe teaches him how to speak English, how to speak European. He is both nameless and languageless, a prime and perhaps necessary illustration of the contemporaneous epistemological concept of human beginning, of the beginning to be human, of the threshold to the human: the Enlightenment's famous *tabula rasa*.

The next symbolic gesture Crusoe manifests is *placing* Friday on his island. He gives him *a place to live*. "The next day after I came home to my hutch with him, I began to consider where I should lodge him; and that I might do well for him, and yet be perfectly easy myself. I made a little tent for him in the vacant place between my two fortifications, in the inside of the last and in the outside of the first." In Crusoe's double-walled castle Friday shall have his place not wholly inside the center with Crusoe, nor wholly outside the center with nature and the other beasts and cannibals, but inside the outside and outside the inside. The Other is made into a subject of possible interaction by being inscribed in the interstices of two symbolic circles.

Finally, Friday is seen as being awestruck by Crusoe's gun, "and I believe if I would have let him, he would have worshipped me and my gun. As for the gun itself, he would not so much as touch it for several days after; but would speak to it and talk to it as if it had answered him when he was by himself; which, as I afterwards learned of him, was to desire it not to kill him" (Defoe 1961:208). Friday, the domesticated Other, the Other already within the range of Western knowledge—understood, classified, explained—would have worshipped Crusoe and his gun had Crusoe allowed him. There is operative here an implicit definition of the Other's religion, his mode of religious practice and belief, and his god—and, by implication, of Crusoe's religion and god. Friday would worship the gun and by extension its owner because it is miraculous to him. The miraculous is what provokes and evokes worship and religion. One can perhaps hear the very distant echoes of Christ's miracles here and the worshippers they gained him. For Crusoe, for the Puritan eighteenth century, at the heart of the religious lies not the sacred but the miraculous, not the solemn stillness of the sacred but the emotional astonishment of the miraculous. In the very first few months of Crusoe's stay on his island something very strange occurs: he suddenly notices next to his hut in the middle of this tropical island a few stalks of barley corn growing. Crusoe is thunderstruck:

> It is impossible to express the astonishment and confusion of my thoughts on this occasion. I had hitherto acted on no religious foundation at all; indeed I had very few notions of religion in my head, nor had entertained any sense of anything that had befallen me, otherwise than as a chance, or, as we lightly say, what pleases God; without so much as inquiring into the end of Providence in these things, or His order in governing events in the world. But after I saw barley grow there, in a climate which I know is not proper for corn, and especially that I knew not how it came there, it startled me strangely, and I began to suggest that God had miraculously caused this grain to grow without any help of seed sown, and

that it was so directed purely for my sustenance on that wild miserable place. This touched my heart a little and brought tears out of my eyes, and I began to bless myself, that such a prodigy of Nature should happen upon my account. . . . (Defoe 1961:60)

We glimpse here for a moment a great rent along one of the newer and weaker seams in the fabric of eighteenth-century rationalism in which Crusoe, as in a tent, has hitherto housed himself. Hippolyte Taine in his brilliant *History of English Literature* (1864) has acutely remarked of Crusoe that "Religion appears, as it must, in emotions and vision: for this is not a calm soul; imagination breaks out into it at the least shock, and carries it to the threshold of madness" (Taine 1965:198). Counterbalancing this almost medieval apocalyptical tendency to religious frenzy, Crusoe displays, especially in the episode where he suddenly spies a single footprint, a desperate and almost titanic will to maintain the sovereignty of his rationalism, his faith. The seam rent by the barley "miracle" is soon hastily resewn and the unstable calm of the homogenous fabric of rationalism is restored. Crusoe sees he can explain this miracle, or, rather, from the perspective of rationalism, this mystery: "At last it occured to my thoughts that I had shook a bag of chicken's feed in that place, and then the wonder began to cease; and I must confess my religious thankfulness to God's Providence began to abate too upon discovering that all this was nothing more but what was common."

The miraculous—that which in its blatant and manifest incomprehensibility produces awe—which threatened to rent Crusoe's world of rationalism, must be, Crusoe assumes, a constitutive part of Friday's world. The gun is permanently for him what the corn was momentarily for Crusoe. The other's religion is identical with Crusoe's but misplaced, misplaced as to the miraculous, as to the gods. The locus of continuity between Crusoe's religion and the "savages" is located along the threshold of the miraculous: their threshold of the miraculous is, in comparison to Crusoe's exceedingly low. (This notion of a low threshold of the miraculous, of a seemingly childish lack of restraint, lack of strength regarding the credulous, will become an indispensable tool for locating the "primitive" in nineteenth-century anthropology.)

Death, the power to produce and distribute death is also, according to Crusoe's definition, central to the religion of the savages; it will provoke their worship, and hence, by referential implication, it is central to the possibilities inherent in Crusoe's concept of religion and worship. A god is he who has the power to unexplainably, yet directly, occasion the death of an other, not he who is perceived as killing in a natural sense, but he who can in an unnatural, incomprehensible sense cause the death of an other.

For Crusoe it is not *time*, as in nineteenth-century evolutionary anthropology, but *religion* that stands between himself and the Other; not historical time but geographical religion, not linear time but spatial religion. Crusoe's desert island is situated in a Christian geography. In terms of longitude and latitude the earth's surface lies first and foremost under the grid of Christian concerns; the geography of the world lies embedded in moral and religious coordinates. After the first violently disturbing confrontation with the human remains of the cannibal's feast Crusoe recovers himself and heartily thanks his God that he was born in the area of the good: "When I came a little out of that part of the island, I stood still a while as amazed, and then recovering myself, I looked with the utmost affliction of my soul, and with a flood of tears in my eyes, gave God thanks that had cast my first lot in a part of the world where I was distinguished from such dreadful creatures as these." (Defoe 1961:163). Crusoe locates this island then, as distinct from the island of England, of Europe, of Christendom, in the dark and dangerous region of this geography of evil.

For Crusoe the "savages" are naked and he is clothed, they are naked and he is armed with a gun, they are naked and he wears Christianity in his soul. The Other is not the primitive; the Other is the savage. It is within a Christian–religious perception that the Other emerges and, for Crusoe, within a national–natural law perspective that he departs and, with Friday, within a domesticated servant position within colonialism, that he remains. For Crusoe the savage does not make essential reference to the time of history, as he will in the nineteenth century, but, rather, to the absence of Christianity and the concomitant nadir of human nature imperceptibly shading off into the beastial and the diabolical, the infernal. In the latter part of the eighteenth century and on into the nineteenth century all this changes: the Other is deployed no longer in a religious space but within a linear anthropological time. With Rousseau's Child of Nature, with Chateaubriand's Noble Savage, with Melville's and Gaugin's Polynesians the Other is perceived as beyond the corruption of the time of history, illustrating, by absence, its alienation; or conversely, with Comte, with Tylor and with Morgan the Other, the Primitive, is perceived within the progress of the time of history, illustrating its retardations, its fossils.

> The conditions necessary for the appearance of an object of discourse, the historical conditions required if one is to "say something" about it, and if several people are to say different things about it, the conditions necessary if it is to exist in relation to other objects, if it is to establish with them relations of resemblance, proximity, distance, difference, transformation—as we can see, these conditions are many and imposing. Which means that one cannot speak of anything at any time. (Foucault 1972:44)

It is not because in the nineteenth century men suddenly looked harder, more objectively, or that they were less blinded by the age-old prejudices of Christianity that they "discovered" that many non-Europeans were actually "primitives," actually represented and represented life in the past, in an age prior to the advent and progress of civilization, in prehistory. Crusoe's savages are not in the same universe as Tylor's primitives. Defoe's Crusoe is not blinded to the truth of the non-Europeans by his Christianity (or by his "culture" as the twentieth century might say), and neither Comte nor Morgan are suddenly freed from the distortion of Christian spectacles, christian a prioris, freed to see, finally, the non-Europeans as what they really are, as "Primitives" (or, as twentieth-century democratic anthropology would have it, as "culturally different"). Crusoe is not blinded by the canons of eighteenth-century Christianity, but rather this Christianity serves as the plane of emergence upon which the Other can appear and be described and deployed in a system of knowledge, i.e., can be related not to "history" or to "progress" or to the "origins of society" as in the nineteenth century, nor to "culture" as in the twentieth century, but to the "diabolical," to "theodicy," and to "nature."

The *truth* of the savages, the cannibals, is that either God allows them or condemns them to *live in falseness*, to live a cruel, barbarous, unholy life. In the Enlightenment, as we shall more and more come to see, the *truth* of the non-European Other is that he *manifests the false*, he makes manifest true ignorance and error,

52

true unenlightenment. For Crusoe it is a rationalized Christianism, Protestantism, that makes available the principles and rules by which the "savages" can be seen and interpreted. They are only visible through Christianity as being the kind of beings that they are: a race of men bereft of God, hence extremely vulnerable to and also probably to a large extent ruled by Satanic forces. The principle topic of conversation and education between Crusoe and Friday is religion, and before all else Crusoe's religion offers the principles that are able and sufficient *to explain* and reduce Friday's cannibal, savage religion. The principle function and sign of the truth of Christianity is that it explains the falsity of the Other's difference. The god of Friday's cannibal tribe is no doubt an apparition of the devil, and their "holy men," who are the only ones allowed to directly speak with their god , reveal the insidious universality of priestcraft and all its attendant immoralities and frauds. It is in a thoroughly Christian space that all the strange and exotic topics of conversation and knowledge are deployed, described, arranged, and finally explained.

In all spheres save one Friday is successfully constrained in and confined to his identity as a being oscillating between the poles of instrumentality and domestic animality. In one area only does he burst the chains of this enforced identity assuming suddenly the authoritative status of a subject questioning Crusoe. That area is, significantly, in the sense, the rationality, of Crusoe's Christian faith. It is here that Friday suddenly manifests the power of interrogation and through this power comes the occasion through which Crusoe learns more about his own Christian faith:

After this, I had been telling him how the devil was God's enemy in the hearts of men, and used all his malice and skill to defeat the good designs of Providence. . . . "But," says he, "if God much strong, much might as the devil, why God no kill the devil so make him no more wicked?" I was strangely surprised at his question. . . . And at first I could not tell what to say; so I pretended not to hear him, and asked him to repeat what he said. But he was too earnest for an answer to forget his question. . . . I had, God knows, more sincerity than knowledge in all the methods I took for this poor creature's instruction, and must acknowledge what I believe all that act upon the same principle will find, that in laying things open to him, I really informed and instructed myself in many things that either I did not know or had not fully considered before, but which occurred naturally to my mind upon my searching into them for the information of this poor savage . . . so that whether this poor wild wretch was the better for me or no, I had great reason to be thankful that ever he came to me. (Defoe 1961:215)

It is with respect to the Christian religion that Friday is able to assume a role somewhat similar to the Socratic interlocutor, raising authoritative questions that produce an acute awareness in Crusoe of his lack of knowledge, of his ignorance, and hence paving the way to the acquisition of a deeper knowledge.

When it comes to the ultimate treatment of the Other, murder, Crusoe expends much thought:

While I was making this march, my former thoughts returning, I began to abate my resolution. I did not mean that I entertained any fear of their number; for a they were naked, unarmed wretches, 'tis certain I was superior to them; nay, though I had been alone; but it occurred to my thoughts what call, what occasion, much less what necessity, I was in to go and dip my hands in blood, to attack people who had neither done or intended me any wrong; who, as to me, were innocent and whose barbarous customs were their own disaster, being in them a token indeed of God's having left them, with the other nations of that part of the world to such stupidity and to such inhuman courses; but did not call me to take upon me to be a judge of their actions, much less an executioner of His justice; that whenever He thought fit, He would take the cause into His own hands, and by national vengeance punish them as a people for national crimes; but that, in the meantime, it was none of my business; that it was true, Friday might justify it, because he was a declared enemy, and in a state of war with those very particular people; and it was lawful for him to attack them; but I could not say the same with respect to me (Defoe 1961:228).

Crusoe doesn't think it's lawful for him, as it would be for Friday, to attack these cannibals as they are a sovereign nation. We witness here, in this encounter, one of the early formulations of the great principle of laissez faire in "inter-national" relations and in eighteenth-century capitalism (it's none of Crusoe's "business"). The principle is altered slightly in its external application, becoming, in respect of international law rather than intranational law, the principal of noninterference in the internal affairs of another na tion. Indeed the moral-legal concept of noninterference and the legal-moral concept of the "nation" are two sides of the same coin. Crusoe suppresses a direct confrontation with Otherness into the framework of the proper interaction of units in a totality as presented to the synoptic gaze, i.e., God's position. It is no longer a primordially direct and in principle principleless (lawless) encounter with the alien Other, but rather now the lawful interaction of a self and a familier other as seen from without and above, from the totalizing perspective of a third party.

CHRISTIANITY, RELIGION AND ANTHROPOLOGY

At the end of the Enlightenment, as Foucault maintains, philosophy *became* anthropology. One of the principle stimuli that prepared and contributed to this historical metamorphosis occurred in the region that we today term "religion." To put it succinctly, in the Enlightenment "Christianity" became "a religion" and "religion" became "anthropological" (not in the nineteenth century meaning of the term but in the eighteenth century sense of "human nature"). There was—in Bayle, in Fontenelle, in Newton, in Hume, de Brosses, and Boulanger, in Dupuis, and de Gebelin—a pervasive and insistant reduction of religious mystery into anthropology; there occurred a tremendous inflation of that enigmatic figure of knowledge we have come to term "man."

In the mature enlightenment Christianity ceased being the most general coordinating grid from within which and upon which one could both order and account for difference. The ancient patristic demonological theory collapsed, and the mutation of Satan into symbol and of Hell into metaphor left a formidable gap in the West's coordinates of location. Probably the most highly visible representation of this cultural movement is Balthasar Bekker's *De Betoverde Weereld* (The World Enchanted, 1693), where Bekker casts "the Devil" out of reality and undertakes to systematically disenchant the world. The economic function of "the Devil" in accounting for difference—the difference of the contemporary non-Christian, and

55

of the ancient pagan—drifted out of the world-horizon, and, in accordance with the dialectic of the Enlightenment (Horkheimer and Adorno 1972), that function became occupied by "Ignorance" (Unenlightenment). For it was *in man's relation to truth* (light) at the same time as it was in the obscuring of that relation to truth (and not, as in the nineteenth century, in man's relation to historical or cultural "stages of development") that the Enlightenment *located and accounted for Difference.* It was in that terrain that the Enlightenment constructed and practiced its "anthropology." Within its organization of knowledge and from its very inception, the Enlightenment's construction of the "primitive mentality" was based on its equivalency to being a "psychology of error." Enlightenment "anthropology" is a "psychology of error," as Renaissance "anthropology" had been a "demonology." As Fontenelle said,

> Madmen we are, but not quite on the pattern of those who are shut up in a madhouse. It does not concern any of them to discover what sort of madness afflicts his neighbor, or the previous occupants of his cell; but it matters very much to us. The human mind is less prone to go astray when it gets to know to what extent, and in how many directions it is itself liable to err, and *we can never devote too much time to the study of our aberrations.* (Hazard 1935:52)

Also Pierre Bayle's project for his dictionary was woven around the concern for a "psychology of error." In a letter to his cousin in 1692 Bayle wrote, "Somewhere about the month of December, 1690, I conceived the idea of compiling a critical dictionary, i.e., a dictionary which should comprise a complete inventory, as it were, of the various errors perpetrated, not only by lexicographers, but by writers in general."

It is at this juncture that we can locate a radical transformation of the West's self-understanding: the European-Christians-and-Jews-as-opposed-to-the-savage-idolatrous-non-Christians became the civilized-Europeans-as-opposed-to-the-superstitous-ignorant-primitive. It was in the Enlightenment, at this epistemological moment, that the European *became civilized* (and since then, on the most primitive level, the West's self-understanding has been absolutely interwoven around its conception of itself as "civilized"). Christianity drastically contracted from being the all pervasive general intellectual horizon upon which difference was experienced and interpreted, and became one element in a more complex general configuration termed "Religion," It was not in the grey dawn of paleolithic man, but in the Enlightenment that "religion" first emerged. In the Enlightenment "religion" was first constituted as a general category, i.e., "religion" became a concept detached from Christianity, from Christianism, and, in an oedipal-like operation, usurped its place. Christianity ceased being the genus, ceased to invisibly yet absolutely mark the parameters of the world, as Febvre's classic Annals study of Rabelais (1947) has shown; now, for the first time, Christianity became a species of the new genus "religion." In a broad movement—yet one almost exactly parallel to the changing concrete practice toward and the theoretical perception of the madman, from the Renaissance to the Enlightenment (Foucault 1965)—the non-European Other ceased being defined by his exclusion, he ceased prowling about enigmatically *outside* Christian membership, and became instead contained and confined: he became *a member of a non-Christian religion*. The Other was no longer defined in advance by exclusion (the non-Christian) but contained in advance by definition (a member of a non-Christian religion). The charged and complex European experience of the North American Indian most dramatically, and most shamefully, manifests this movement (though later than the eighteenth century) in the transformation from the general policy of Removal (exclusion and annihilation) into the policy of the Reservation System (confinement) (Pearce 1965).

Dialectically, when the Other became a member of a non-Christian religion, the Christian likewise became a member of the Christian religion. Lord Herbert of Cherbury's initial construction in *De Veritate* (1624) and *De Religione Gentilium* (1663), and the continuing elaboration and dissemination of Enlightenment "deism" was a central element in this general intellectual shift. Within this movement "religion" retained for awhile its autonomy and absoluteness as ground—as we shall see with Newton—but soon it itself became grounded in "nature" and "human nature"—as we shall see with Hume. (In the nineteenth century "religion" and "religions" will be re-grounded, as with Feuerbach, in Anthropology).

Though it is little known, much, nay, most of Newton's thinking was passionately engaged in an intellectual movement that has become relatively invisible for the conventional European historical perspective, principally because it was so successful in authoritatively establishing itself as that conventional European historical perspective. Newton was engaged most of his life in that broad European enterprise stretching from the late sixteenth through the early eighteenth century of establishing a *world chronology*. This project was intimately implicated in accounting for the origins of pagan religions, which in its turn was also closely implicated in the *question of the Bible*: the status and place of the Bible in its relation to authoritative knowledge (a question of the gravitational center of authority).

At Leydon Jacob Gronovius asserts that there never was such a person as Romulus, Henry Dodwell, at Oxford, also expresses grave doubts about him. . . . It is certain that with the exception of Holy Writ, there is no history which does not partake of the fabulous in its earliest beginnings. The history of Rome before the time of Romulus is unworthy of credit, and even the story of Romulus is perhaps open to doubt. . . . As for the history of Greece . . . it was even more untrustworthy than the Roman. . . . All their dates and periods are a hopeless tangle. . . . Well then, let us put profane history aside and let us concentrate on the one history that really matters, the history dictated by God. Here all is plain sailing; from the creation of the world to the coming of Christ there is an interval of 4,000 years. . . . By the year 129 the population of the earth had considerably increased. . . . In the year 1636, came the Flood; in 1757, men set to work to build the Tower of Babel. . . . Thanks to these firmly established landmarks, Bossuet, composing his noble *Discours sur l'Histoire Universelle* beholds a succession of epochs which automatically fall into their appointed places in the great scheme of things. . . . And then, over against these innocent beliefs, this tranquil peace of mind, loomed up the figure of Chronology. At first sight it seemed no more than a mild discipline. . . . However, in proportion as the suspicion of confusion in the records of humanity gained ground, so also did the status and reputation of Chronology. It was recognized as an indispensable branch of knowledge. . . . Just as the art of navigation furnishes pilots with rules for sailing the sea without wandering from their course, however long the voyage, so are we indebted to Chronology for the skill to find our way with certainty over the vast and shadowy realms of the past. (Hazard 1935:39)

58

In the year 1700 chronology was still *the* central problem of universal history: "The masse of Histories would prove but a confused heape, and be like a Monster if Chronology did not help to form and frame them into a fashion, by digesting them into a certainetie of articulate times. And lastly, it is termed the Soul of History giving life to it, as the Soul doth to the body." So wrote Henry Isaacson, a "chronologist" of the seventeenth century with whom Newton was familiar. Chronology at this time was firmly *Biblical* chronology, *Christian* chronology.

> The major Christian chronologists of the 16th century and 17th century had firmly established Hebrew history as the axis of world chronology, since the Biblical genealogies from Adam down presented them with a continuous reckoning in years unique among ancient historical records. . . . Scaliger, Petau, Ussher, Marsham, and Dodwell—to mention only the grand masters of the art—were all in substantial agreement with computations based on the Old Testament which proved that the world was about four or five thousand years old at the birth of Christ. (Manuel 1963:38)

The intervals from Adam through Noah, through Abraham, through the Babylonian Captivity on through Christ were the basic units of seventeenth-century chronological discourse.

The problem of history for the philosophy of the Enlightenment arises in the field of religious phenomena. It is here that this problem first became urgent (Cassirer 1955:195). The early Enlightenment attempt to establish a world chronology was an attempt to establish a unity, to forcefully establish one world, one temporally homogenous order within which comparisons and evaluations could be made. The task, as visible in the works of Scaliger and Isaacson, and later, in Nicholas Freret and Newton, was to synchronize all the various histories of the ancient peoples that were at hand into one overall arching unity, one common, communal and omni-inclusive stream of time: one world. "World history" means "one history"; and the possibility of establishing a "world history" presupposed the prior secure establishment of a "world chronology." (In another sense, it presupposed the constitution of the coordinating order of the great European archive within which and upon whose documents world history may unfold and manifest itself.) Newton's main work, *The Chronology of the Ancient Kingdoms Amended* (1728), both displayed and participated in the central problematic of this movement: "The really thorny problem was to synchronize the events reported in Egyptian, Assyrian, Babylonian, Persian, Greek, and Roman annals with Biblical history" (Manuel 1963:40).[1] This enterprise also included the initial attempts to establish "connections" with Chinese history, Indian history, and other exotic peoples whose records were being introduced into Europe. It was an attempt to integrate the records of the various extant histories into one unified and unifying general order within the circumference of the European archive; to inscribe all the world within the Christian European circle. The various "histories" of the various ancient kingdoms had to be synchronized into "history," and the primary rhythm around and through which they were to be interwoven in "connections" and synchronized into one overall unitary pattern was Biblical history: a somewhat tyrannical synthesis willed and guided by the ideal of a totalitarian unity.[2]

The establishment of Christian chronology as the yardstick, as the standard by which any other chronology could be evaluated and either forcefully integrated or forcefully excluded and judged false and chimerical, was an attack against the autonomy of the pagan worlds; an attempt to tyrannically integrate them into a Christian world:[3]

> Newton's zeal in demolishing the inflated claims of Greeks, Romans, Egyptians, Chaldeans, Persians, and Chinese was sparked by diverse purposes; . . . by all odds the most deep rooted of his motives was a defense of the Hebrew scriptural tradition and Jewish antiquities against the new libertines who were extolling the pagan Ancients at Israel's expense. Not only was the Bible the most authentic history in the world, but the kingdom of Israel was the first large-scale political society with all the attributes of civilization. (Manuel 1963:89)

The primordial chronology, the *fundamental calendar* upon which the other chronologies were to find their space and be inserted in their place was the ancient Jewish-Christian chronology. Throughout this early Enlightenment enterprise of making *one* history "Biblical chronology remained the touchstone, incontrovertible, by which all heathen chronologies were to be tested" (Manuel 1963:49). The space, the "neutral chronology" in which history, "world history," can unfold and flow was always already a Biblical space; the "blank-paged book" of chronology upon which the narrative of world history could thenceforth be written already had a Biblical binding. "The rise of modern anthropology is inseparable from the emergence of new conceptions of Time in the wake of a thorough secularization of the Judeo-Christian idea of history. The transformation that occured involved, first, a generalization of historical Time, its extension, as it were, from the circum-Mediterranean stage of events to the whole world" (Fabian 1983:146). The Bible was not a centrally important text *in* history, but rather the very ground and horizon upon which Enlightenment "history" took on the structuring and ordering it did take on. The Bible gives place to the unfolding of history; Biblical chronology makes history possible, makes the ordering that history presupposes possible.

PROPHECY AND PREDICTION: THE STATUS OF THE BIBLE

As Newton shaped the main anatomical ligaments of "world history" around the skeletal structure of the Hebrew-Christian Bible, so too, a central anatomical feature of his "empirical science" was stretched out along that same skeletal structure. The centrality and uniqueness of the Bible assumed by much of Enlightenment "history" and, in at least one aspect, by "empirical science," was also contested by much of Enlightenment "philosophy," especially the "rationalists." Spinoza, perhaps, best represented the contesting position of seeing the Bible in its relation to knowledge: "I may sum up the matter by saying that the method of interpreting Scripture does not widely differ from the method of interpreting nature—in fact, it is almost the same" (Spinoza 1965:99). This principle, so seemingly simple, was yet, as Cassirer says in his *Philosophy of the Enlightenment*,

> so decisive and far reaching in its consequences; being, or the nature of things [or "world history"] is not to be understood through the Bible, but the Bible itself is to be understood as a portion of this being, and therefore as subject to its general laws. The Bible is not the key to nature [world history] but part of it; it must therefore be considered according to the same rules as hold for any kind of empirical knowledge. (Cassirer 1955:186)[4]

The status, place, and value of the Bible, in its relation to knowledge, was very different for the "rationalist" Spinoza than for the "empiricist" Newton. Newton (a Puritan) applied a Biblical criticism to the credibility of pagan historical testimonies (and thereby constituted the primacy and firstness of Jewish-Christian civilization and of monotheism), while Spinoza (a Jew) forged a historical criticism of Biblical testimonies. For Spinoza, the universal rules of knowledge were applicable in undertaking to know the Bible as they were for any other concrete topic of study. For Newton this was not the case.

> For Newton the most compelling proofs of the intimacy of God's relations with His creatures were to be discovered in history, not in "theology" and "vain philosophy." . . . Religious truth was determined by the accuracy of prophetic transmission, not by metaphysical arguments; . . . the real evidences of Christianity, for Newton as for divines and Fathers of the Church extending back to Augustine, were historical: the narration of true events, witnessed, and the demonstration of true prophecy. (Manuel 1963:9)[5]

Contrary to the position represented by Spinoza, for Newton the Bible, rather, was the authoritative *source* from which derived universal rules of knowledge—rules applicable to any concrete empirical topic of study:

> The Book of Daniel and the Apocalypse of St. John, Newton showed, were prophetic historical statements which had proved to be factually true down to the minutest detail; they had predicted, described in advance, the early history of Christianity and the history of the great post-Biblical monarchies. The fulfillment of Prophecy in history was always one of the most convincing proofs of the truth of religion in both the Jewish and Christian traditions. . . . In the *Observations Upon the Prophecies* Newton demonstrated that they had been abundantly fulfilled in Eastern European history, by spelling out the specific events, complete with geographic locations, names of kings, dates of battles, and revolutions of empires, to which they correspond. (Manuel 1963:144)

This is all to say one thing: the *social authority* and *psychological force* of modern empirical scientific "prediction" *grew out of* archaic Christian roots; in this sense, science, as Nietzsche has extensively analyzed, is directly derived from Christianity in that the form supporting scientific belief is derived from the form supporting Christian belief. Absolutely central to what constituted the authority of the Protestant's (Puritan's) Bible was also what was absolutely central to what constituted the authority of the Protestant's scientific knowledge: prophecy and its fulfillment: prediction and its verification. Theories, in order to be "scientific," must have observable consequences, predictable consequences (Popper 1968). The authority of knowledge that is grounded upon prediction is an analogical derivative of the authority of Christianity that is grounded upon prophecy. For Newtonian "empirical science" in general, and, by implication, for most modern science, the authority of knowledge is grounded on its interdependence with prediction and this interdependence, this necessary complicity, was analogically derived from the authority of Christian faith grounded upon its interdependency with prophecy. Modern scientific "prediction" was a dialectical secularization of Christian "prophecy"— simultaneously denying and preserving it. Which is to say modern scientific "prediction" presupposes and preserves Christianity, it is a *secularization* of Christianity, and is not a return or a renaissance of classical Greek science with its natural prognostications and natural consequences:

> The fact that Polybius felt no difficulty in prognosticating future developments indicates the fundamental difference between the classical and the Christian outlook and attitude in regard to the future. To Polybius, it was "an easy matter" to foretell the future "by inference from the past." To the Old Testament writers only the Lord himself could reveal, through his prophets, a future which is independent of all that has happened in the past, and which cannot be inferred from the past as a natural consequence. Hence, the fulfillment of prophecies as understood by the Old and New Testament writers is entirely different from the verification of prognostications concerning historiconatural events. Though the future may be predetermined by the will of God, it is determined by a personal will and not by a natural fatality, and man can never fortell it unless God reveals it to him. And . . . the basic feeling in regard to the future becomes one of suspense in the face of its theoretical incalculability (Löwith 1949:9)

The unique authority of "successful prediction" was a secularization of "successful prophecy," prophecy fulfilled. A scientific prediction, a saying in advance, is constituted at the heart of Newtonian empirical science as a miniature prophecy, a secular prophecy wherein a scientific knower aided by his scientific knowledge—rather than a prophet inspired by his God—says in advance what will take place, and the verification of the prediction is like the fulfillment of the prophecy that thereby and therewith convinces others (and self) of its hitherto unsubstantiated claim (as hypothesis) to truth and its hitherto unrecognized claim to authority. To predict in advance, to prophesize, is a great form of authority in the Christian-secular tradition of the west.

THE ORIGIN OF PAGAN RELIGIONS

In 1700 a great perplexity began once again to weigh heavily on the horizon of European identity: a perplexity, an enigma, obsessively demanding attention; an enigma that until then had laid long dormant, covered over by the blanket of Christian faith: *How and why did ancient pagan religions arise?* What was the origin, what was the cause of pagan religions? And, in close proximity, *How did all these strange, savage, non-European religions arise?* What is the cause of these proliferating idolatries?

For Newton the origin of these pagan religions was to be found in their degeneration from the original biblical monotheistic faith. This "degeneration" was already beginning to be "anthropological" with Newton in that it was no longer fundamentally attributed to demonic powers but was now seen as the result of human powers: this marked, in one sense, what we may call the humanization of the demonic, the anthropologization of the demonic. It is here, in this area, that we may reconstruct the specific meaning of "euhemerism" and "anthropomorphism" as Enlightenment accounts of difference.[6]

In contrast to Bishop Warburton's *Divine Legation of Moses* (1738), Voltaire announced in his *Philosophical Dictionary* (1764):

Another, much more philosophical scholar, who is one of the most profound metaphysicians of our times [Hume] gives powerful reasons to prove that polytheism was mankind's first religion, and that several gods were first believed in before reason was enlightened enough not to recognize more than one supreme being. I venture to think, on the contrary, that men first acknowledged a single god, and that *human weakness* later adopted several. . . . (Voltaire 1971:350)

The debate raged with remarkable stability from one end of the Enlightenment to the other,[7] it was born with the Enlightenment and more or less died with it (when the conditions that made it possible, the epistemological network, altered): Which was first, polytheism or monotheism? Was polytheism a degeneration of primitive biblical monotheism (Newton), or, perhaps, of an original, natural deism (Churbury, Toland, Voltaire, all the deists)? Or, on the contrary, was polytheism the first "natural religion" and monotheism the later result of the slow laborious ascent of abstraction toward truth (fragile and ever reversible with Hume, solid and inevitable with Turgot and Condorcet)?

"For the moral law observed by all nations while they lived together in Chaldea under the governance of Noah and his sons and afterwards by the Chaldeans, Canaanites, and Hebrews and till they began to worship their dead kings required the worship of one supreme God" (Newton as quoted in Manuel 1963:112). According to Newton, originally all mankind had been believers in the one true God. The task of the Newtonian reconstruction of ancient history and chronology was to account for polytheism from the perspective of the truth of Christian monotheism. Unlike the Renaissance, Newton, within the Enlightenment, accounted for the *error of idolatry* from the perspective of the *truth of Biblical revelation*. We may say of Enlightenment "idolatry"—that primary property and insignia by which human difference is constituted and recognized in Newton's world—what Foucault says of madness as it was experienced by the Age of Reason: "Idolatry" for Newton begins where the relation of man to truth is disturbed and darkened. It is in this relation, at the same time as in the destruction of this relation, that "idolatry" assumes its general meaning and its particular forms. It constitutes, on the one hand, primarily a version of human forgetfulness, a slow drift into darkness, error, oblivion. The ancient pagan and the non-European "idolaters" are those who have forgotten and drifted into ignorance. And on the other hand, it constituted a visible sign of man's capacity for deliberate political perversion. Men have been duped by their kings. The rulers and "priests" have deliberately spread ignorance and darkness in order to sustain and ever strengthen their political power and political order.

The origin of pagan religions? "For what else were the gods of the Greeks but their ancient kings?" (Newton). Newton had to derive polytheism, idolatry, from monotheism (Hume will reverse this and arrive at monotheism by progressively transcending polytheism), and his principle method was that common to the community of historians of ancient times in the seventeenth and eighteenth centuries, namely *euhemerism*. In Newton's words:

> In the religion propagated from Noah and his sons men worshipped one God with prayers and praises and giving of thanks accompanied with significant ceremonies, such as were sacrifices and thanksgiving for benefits received, or prayer for pardon of offences and other benefits desired. . . . Upon ye first peopling of the earth every family traveling from place to place carried with them a sacred fire for sacrifice, the father of the family being as well priest or king. Whence it became the customs of all nations to keep perpetual fires in their sacred places. The Jews did it in their temples. The Egyptians and Chaldeans in theirs, Persians in their Pyrethra and the cities of the Greeks and Latines in their Prytanea and Vestal Temples. The sacrifices of ye first nations were vegetables fit for food and clean beasts and birds. For the distinction of beasts into clean and unclean was as old as ye days of Noah. Of vegetables the first fruits and tenths were God's lot and of animals first born. And this seems to have been the religion of ye world before the rise of Idolatry. But after cities began to unite into kingdoms the people began to flatter their kings and at length to carry on the flattery of them after death by supposing that their souls survived and resided about their graves and sepulchers and grave stones and could do men good and hurt and on that account began to invoke them and build altars to them and worship them with oblations and sacrifices and at length to worship the stones themselves as inhabited by these feigned deities. And at length when men grew skillful in carving and building figures they made the images of the kings and building sepulchers in ye form of Temples, set up the Images in ye Temples and worshipped them as inhabited by the souls of ye dead kings. (Manuel 1963:114)

The truth of the priority of Biblically revealed monotheism was assumed, and what was problematic, what called for and called forth an account, was the lapse into idolatry, i.e., into error. Idolatry was a human perversion, a distortion of the truth of primitive, universal Biblical monotheism. In this sense, the task of Newtonian "anthropology" was, in the deepest sense, the Enlightenment formulation of a *psychology of error*. In respect to the anthropo morphic Greco-Roman gods this manifested itself in the tendency to transfigure heros and apotheosize kings; in respect to the bizarre "animal gods" of the ancient Egyptians (and the savage non-Europeans) this manifested itself in theriomorphic gods, in zoolatry, again, the tendency to divinize great kings, but indirectly through an iconographic language, i.e., hieroglyphics, of animal emblems.

Euhemerism was central to the "anthropology" of the Age of Reason; it marked an attempt to reduce myth to history, the mythical to the historical, as is vividly illustrated in Antoine Banier's *The Mythology and Fables of the Ancients Explained from History (1740)*. It refused to see in ancient myths the mythological and firmly persevered in the attempt to see in myths a human distortion of the historical and the commonsensical. Euhemerism was a rereading of the Ancient's myths—a rereading wholly unlike the Renaissance's—which galvanized its attention on any and every element that appeared to transcend the natural order of terrestrial life— the Enlightenment's "natural order"—in order to contest and then finally reduce it to being another instance in conformity with that order. It constituted a single-minded effort at universal unification. Enlightenment "euhemerism" was the structural reversal of Enlightenment "anthropomorphism." As Gadamer says of Betti's psychological hermeneutics, "In the process of interpretation we are concerned with a reversal or inversion of the creative process "(Gadamer 1975:465), so we may say that euhemerism was an inversion of "creative" anthropomorphism; it represented a looking at anthropomorphism backwards, in a reverse movement. Euhemerism represented the tyrannical effort that saw, interpreted, and made common sense of the strangeness, difference, bizarreness, and otherness of ancient pagan myths and idolatrous practices by means of pragmatizing those myths and practices. Euhemerism, as a general Enlightenment category, was an interpretive strategy formulated against the archaic authority of a demonical world; a strategy formulated against the sixteenth century's patristic demonological theory of idolatry. The Others, the ancient pagans,

the living savages, are no longer linked to the world and its subterranean demonological forms. They are now linked to man, to
his moral weakness and intellectual distortions, i.e., they are fundamentally linked to *error and ignorance*.

THE ANCIENTS AND THE OTHER

It began around 1700 and continued with great vitality through
the entire century. In 1700 Père Noel Alexandre published his *Con-
formité des ceremonies chinoises avec l'idolatrie grecque et romaine*.
A few years later in 1704 M. de la Créquinière wrote *The Agreement
of the Customs of the East Indians with those of the Jews, and the
Other Ancient Peoples: being the first essay of this kind, towards the
explaining of several difficult passages in Scripture, and some of the
most Ancient writers, by present Oriental Customs* (Eng. trans. 1705).
In 1724 Pierre Joseph Lafitau, the Jesuit missionary to America,
brought out his illustrated *Moeurs des savages Ameriquains com-
parée aux moeurs des premiers temps*. In 1760 Charles de Brosses
wrote *Le Culte des dieux fetiches or Parallèle de l'ancienne religion
de l'Egypt avec la religion actuelle de Negritie*. And, at century's end,
in 1799, Joseph Priestly published his *Comparison of the institutions of Moses with those of the Hindoos and the other ancient nations*. In the Enlightenment the Other re-presents the Ancient. How
is this possible?

Enlightenment philosophy, beginning with Descartes, dividing
into the empiricist and the rationalist traditions, and reintegrating
with Kant, is above all, a philosophy of representation (Foucault
1970) tightly and densely wound around the "epistemological
problem" of determining how representation could be linked to
what it represented, how to represent representation. In its initial
explorations and investigations of the non-European, or, rather, non-
Enlightened world, the Enlightenment at first encountered mostly
"the savage" the "barbarian," and the "idolatrous semicivil" of the
East. Then in a complex, obscure and confusing modification, the
savage as he was mixed with the *ancients* (pagans and Jews) became the *primitive*. The savage took on the value and the status of
representing the ancients. La Créquinière emphasized to his readers
that the study of the "customs of the Indians is no ways useful
itself, that I thought myself oblig'd to make use of it, only to justify
what is told us of the Ancients, and to explain it wherever the oc-

casion offers, and, in a word, that Antiquity was my only aim" (La Créquinière 1705:7). As the non-European became the representation of the Ancients, he simultaneously became the primitive. He came to represent and re-present the Ancients not in accordance with a proto nineteenth century evolutionary-anthropological perspective, as a "survival" of past "stages of development," but more in accordance with an Enlightenment philosophical theory of representation.

> The Past abandoned, the Present enthroned in its place! Yet another transition! How are we to account for it? How came it that a whole section of Europe's intelligentsia suddenly dropped the cult of antiquity, which the Renaissance and the classical age so consistently professed? The famous battle between the ancients and the moderns, which is commonly advanced in explanation of the phenomenon, is, in fact, but a symptom of it. (Hazard 1954:30)

Bayle (1697) and Fontenelle (1724), Locke (1695 and 1696) and Hume (1757), Newton and Freret (1726), Montesquieu (1721 and 1758) and Voltaire (1733, 1764 and 1766), all participated in the general Enlightenment reappraisal of pagan antiquity (Gay 1966), all participated in and fostered the general devaluation of the Renaissance's vision and experience of ancient paganism that was, obversely, the Enlightenment's construction of the pagan-primitive-unenlightened mentality. In one of its central aspects the Enlightenment represented an enormous effort *to see* the ancients—the Egyptians, the Jews, the Romans, above all the Greeks—*as* pagan-primitives, *as* savages, and, reciprocally, to see the newly established contemporary savages of the travel literature *as similar* to the pagan ancients. It represented an attempt to homologize the difference of the "ancients" with that of the heathen savages:

> Unknowing supporters of this enterprise were the travel writers who had explored the dark continents of the world and the brave missionaries to the modern heathens—Abraham Roger, La Créquinière, Richard Blone, Joannes Schefferus, Arnolderus Montanus, Père Charles Le Cebien, William Bosman. Virtually any writing which shed light on "conformities" between Greco-Roman ritual and the religion of contemporaneous heathen societies, whether peoples living in a state of civil-

ity—the Chinese, Hindus, the Persians—or savage Negroes and American Indians, helped fashion the new view of ancient paganism. . . . In the course of time the juxtaposing of ancient and modern cults gave birth to a new perception of Greco-Roman religion. . . . Pagan religion became a living flesh-and-blood reality which was mirrored in contemporary barbarism. The development of this awareness was gradual; . . . not until the last decades of the seventeenth century did the refashioned image of Greco-Roman worship—coarse, crude, primitive, abhorrent, at once fanatical and artificial—emerge as a historical experience of humanity. . . . By the first quarter of the eighteenth century the two paganisms had been completely assimiliated with each other. The parallel always worked both ways: it infused meaning into the savage rites in the new world, and at the same time it became the key to a re-interpretation of the spirit of the ancients. The growing late seventeenth-century perjorative attitude toward paganism, the realization that the Greeks were primitives, was concomitant to the literary quarrel between the ancients and the moderns, that many faceted discussion which served to clear a path for the appearance of the idea of progress. (Manuel 1959:15–19)

What were the epistemological conditions that authorized, for the Enlightenment, the comparability of the ancient pagans and the contemporary non-Europeans? How was it possible to compare them? Way was it "automatic" or "necessary" to see them *as* comparable? What was the good, the purpose, of this tremendous self-defining cultural act of comparison? On what horizon did they emerge in simultaneity for the Enlightenment's gazing and comparing eye? From within the epistemological network of the eighteenth century, "It was virtually impossible to examine a strange, savage religion without noting disparities and conformities with what one knew about ancient paganism" (Manuel 1959:22). How was this analogical space constituted between the ancient Egyptians, Jews, Greeks, and Romans, and the contemporary aliens? How was it possible, or, perhaps, why was it necessary to "spontaneously" *see the analogy*—the similarity and the dissimilarity—between the Greeks and the non-European Other?

It is perhaps in the area where the ancient pagan's "myths and religions" and the contemporary non-European's "myths and religions" come into contact with the modern European's Enlightenment (i.e., with the Enlightenment's version of itself and of its knowledge of knowledge) that our questions will prove the most fruitful; in the area where the *Eighteenth Century Confronts the Gods* (as Manuel's first-rate study is named), where Enlightenment knowledge confronts pagan and primitive ignorance, pagan and primitive "superstition," pagan and primitive Unenlightenment.

In reference to the ancient pagans and the contemporary non-Europeans, the Enlightenment never tires of asking one question over and over again: What is there in the nature of man that has caused him to invent and worship these false gods? What is the origin of Greek and non-European religions? What is the origin of this peculiar manifestation of pagan and primitive ignorance? "Superstition, then, is engendered, preserved, and fostered by fear" (Spinoza 1965:4). And Hume:

> We hang in perpetual suspense between life and death, health and sickness, plenty and want; which are distributed amongst the human species *by secret and unknown causes*, whose operation is oft unexpected, and always unaccountable. These unknown causes, then become the constant object of our hope and fear. . . . Could men anatomize nature, according to the most probable, or at least the most intelligible philosophy, they would find, that these causes are nothing but the particular fabric and structure of the minute parts of their own bodies and of external objects; and that, by a regular and constant machinery, all the events are produced, about which they are so much concerned. But this philosophy exceeds the comprehension of the ignorant multitude, who can only conceive the unknown causes in a general and confused manner. . . . (Hume 1956:28, emphasis mine)

In the Enlightenment the early pagan and the contemporary non-European were fundamentally similar because neither was enlightened, i.e., *neither knew of unknown causes* (this also authorizes their similarity to European peasants and to children). The self-identity of the Enlightenment is aligned with knowledge *as opposed to* the identity of the unenlightened, alien Other that is aligned with ignorance: Enlightenment knowledge consists in awareness of ignorance and ignorance consists of nonawareness of ignorance. *Not knowing about ignorance* is the very being of ignorance. The

71

Ignorance of the Other consists of his ignorance of Ignorance. The alien Others are seen as ignorant because they don't know that they don't know. What they don't know is the nature of ignorance. The Other manifests the incarnation not of sin and Satan but of Ignorance. The nature of ignorance in the Enlightenment *episteme* is not knowing about unknown causes, i.e., that there *are* unknown causes. Not knowing that there are unknown causes of which we are ignorant is the deep nature of Ignorance, of Unenlightenment, of the Other. Neither the early pagans nor the contemporary non-Europeans recognized the reality of the omnipresent operation of unknown causes. Within the Age of Reason, in sharp contrast to the Renaissance, *belief in unknown causes* was the central axis by which science moved,[8] it was a belief that profoundly shaped and authorized the project of modern science:

> The eighteenth century in Europe was the complete antithesis to the Middle Ages; . . . the earlier period was the age of faith based upon reason. In the later period, they let sleeping dogs lie: it was an age of reason based upon faith . . .. St. Anselm would have been distressed if he had failed to find a convincing argument for the existence of god, and on this argument he based his edifice of faith, whereas Hume based his *Dissertation on the Natural History of religion* upon his faith in the order of nature. (Whitehead 1925:57)

"Unknown causes" were necessary and intrinsic to the constitution and continued operation of the scientific method. "Unknown causes" were not unknowable causes, but always, by nature and by necessity, potentially knowable. "Unknown causes" were unknown-causes-that-necessarily-can-gradually-come-to-be-known: It was of the nature of the way his newly constituted scientific method operated that allowed, nay compelled, Descartes in 1637 to say, "So I want it to be understood that the little I have learned thus far is a mere nothing compared to what I do not know and yet do not despair of learning" (Descartes 1961:48). This Enlightenment belief in unknown causes presupposed a belief in causality—as Hume was to show—and also a belief in the necessarily progressive character of human knowledge, i.e., that what is *now* unknown can and will *in the future* come to be known. Condorcet (1794) and Turgot (1750) were later to bring into bold relief the historicality and progressive nature implicit in this conception and organization of knowlege. In the Enlightenment "causes" were of two types in relation to the order of knowledge: known and unknown, or, rather, as-yet-unknown; but of a single uniform type in relation to the order of being: omnipresently there and constantly operative. In the Enlightenment the realm of being is coextensive with the realm of causality (hence Kant's "problem of morality and freedom," i.e., in the Enlightenment "nature" is isomorphic with "causality," nature is coextensive with causality, and one cannot conceive of something that is natural but not deterministic). Progress, therefore, was relatable *only to the order of knowledge* (to transforming "unknowns" into "knowns") and *not to the order of being*—which is to say Enlightenment "progress" is strictly incommensurable with and not a proto "anticipation" of nineteenth-century "evolution." The conventional seeing of Enlightenment "progress" as an anticipation and forerunner of the nineteenth century's concept of evolution is due to the illusion of retrospective historicizing. No conception of "organic development" or of a realist "evolutionary process" was epistemologically possible in the Enlightenment (Lowe 1982).

In the Enlightenment a belief in the reality of causality was the mirror image of a belief in the efficacy of knowledge. *To believe in unknown causes* was to be "Enlightened," to believe in knowledge, rather than "superstition" (again, one can't have unknowable causes as one has already ensnared every thing within the rigid net of mechanical causality). For the Enlightenment *causality was not a particular experience in the world, but rather the way of experiencing the world*. A belief, a *real* belief, in Vaihinger's sense (Vaihinger 1924), in the reality of causality[9]—as Kant was later to show with the concept of the "a priori" in the *Critique of Pure Reason*—was the fundamental basis for the belief in the possibility of knowledge and the possibility of the progress of knowledge (to discover and uncover ever more and more causes ad infinitum). Within this particular intellectual geography the otherness of the Other was to be determined.

Lord Herbert of Cherbury's formulation of deism in *De Religione Gentilium Errorum que opud Eos Causis* (The Ancient Religion of the Gentiles, and the Causes of Their Errors Considered, 1663) may serve as a convenient marker: "the causes of their errors." It was only with the Enlightenment's construction of the concept of "unknown causes" that the myths and religions of the ancient pagans and the contemporary non-Europeans could be seen as ignorance, i.e., as erroneous evaluations of "unknown causes." "Myths" and polytheistic religions were then experienced as errors—for in order to see "myths," both those of the ancients as well as those of the primitives, *as erroneous evaluations of "unknown causes,"* the Enlightenment first had to have the established concept of "unknown causes." The entire global effort of the Enlightenment to explain myths as false explanations (to account for difference as ignorance) radically devalued and transformed the mythological character of myth: "a myth is living or dead, not true or false. You cannot refute a myth because as soon as you treat it as refutable, you do not treat it as a myth but as a hypothesis or history" (MacIntyre 1967:435). For the Enlightenment mythologizing was essentially and unavoidably *false thinking*. There could be no "science of myth" in the nineteenth- and twentieth-century sense because there were no myths, merely false scientific thinking. The Enlightenment tried to pulverize myth back into thought. Hume, Bayle, Fontenelle, Newton all make manifest the Enlightenment psychologization of myth and religion: the seeing of "myths" and of alien "religions" as expressions of the primitive mind of man, false explanations of the order of things. Again, Enlightenment "anthropology" was grounded upon a psychology of error; and what made this possible was the interpretative scheme of "unknown causes," for the Enlightenment had to have an alternative interpretation and explanation of "natural phenomena," and especially of "natural calamities" in order *not* to see the gods at work. Like Robinson Crusoe, constantly on the precarious edge of "enlightened consciousness" the Enlightenment had to vigorously and persistantly "naturalize" phenomena. (This was, perhaps, the underlying meaning of Voltaire's obsessive preoccupation with the Lisbon earthquake and its "justification").

"The pagans always copied their divinities after themselves" (Fontenelle). Whenever the Age of Reason looked at the religions of the ancients and the savage and semicivilized non-Europeans it saw anthropomorphism. "In spite of its professed interest in distant lands and ages, historiography in the Enlightenment was a series of judgments, based on the belief that other ages were either identical with or different from the eighteenth century" (Lowe 1982:42). As Bougainville's savage (Diderot 1772) is different from Bougainville and the Europeans he encounters in that he is incapable of recognizing their difference from himself, so Hume's early barbarous men were different in that they were incapable of recognizing God's difference from themselves—as we nonanthropomorphic European monotheists do. The barbarous ages, the early polytheists, were constitutionally indifferent to God's difference, indifferent to God's otherness.

> There is a universal tendency in mankind to conceive all beings like themselves, and to transfer to every object, those qualities with which they are familiarly acquainted, and of which they are intimately conscious. . . . No wonder then, that mankind, being placed in such an absolute ignorance of causes, and being at the same time so anxious concerning their future fortune, should immediately acknowledge a dependence on invisible powers, possessed of sentiment and intelligence. The *unknown causes* which continually employ their thought . . . are all apprehended to be of the same species. (Hume as quoted in Manuel 1959:173)

The gods of the "primitive mind" were explained by a psychological projection theory. For the Enlightenment, "gods were originally invoked in connection with specific concrete events of life because uninstructed aboriginal man was incapable of an abstract conception of the universe . . ." (Manuel 1959:173), i.e., he was incapable of a *mechanistic* conception of the universe. Newtonian mechanics here reveals itself as the dominant metaphor in retrospectively formulating and describing "primitive mentality"; primitive mentality is that which *lacks* Newtonian mechanism, which is ignorant of a Newtonian mechanistic vision of the general operation of the cosmos. In the Enlightenment, for the first time, *one was able to see anthropomorphism*, i.e., anthropomorphism presupposes mechanism; anthropomorphism became possible only on the horizon of Newtonian mechanism. The critical and criticizing recognition of anthropomorphism presupposed a prior commitment to a general mechanical philosophy of nature, to the mechanistic Newtonian vision of the "life" of the cosmos.

This marks a profound alteration, morally speaking, in our Western experience of the events of nature as now no longer intentional—hence moral and within the sphere, order and rule of justice—but rather fundamentally as statistical. Nature is no longer intentional but statistical, and the events of our life, tragic and painful, happy and beneficial, are not of an intentional order—blessings and curses of the gods—but of a statistical order. Hence a good part of modern philosophical wisdom consists in the attempt and moral intellectual demand to see the events of the cosmos *as statistical rather than as* intentional, as anthropomorphic. As Spinoza teaches, to ask, in the face of a tragic, or beneficial, event, "why?" is to ask a fundamentally false question. It is a question that presses upon us, to be sure, but philosophical wisdom consists in maintaining a position of indifference toward it.

The eighteenth century saw "myths" on the horizon of mathematics, on the horizon of mechanics: it was only possible to psychologize myths, to see them as anthropomorphic projection-explanations on the horizon of a mathematical-mechanical universe. Only when one "observes" myths on a mathematical-mechanical field can they appear as anthropomorphic-psychological projections. Mythopoeic reasoning was not simply "false," "erroneous," it was false mathematical-mechanical reasoning, false abstract reasoning. It was experienced *as false* only insofar as it was judged as failing to be mechanical-mathematical reasoning.

In the Age of Reason not "ignorance" but "ignorance of causes" produced the superstitions of the Other, and not "knowledge" but "knowledge of unknown causes" produced liberation and Enlightenment. "Ignorance of causes" accounted for the difference, the similar difference, of the ancient pagans and the non-European Others from the Enlightenment itself. And, in structural simultaneity, anthropomorphic psychology produced the visibility of their similarity, i.e., provided the epistemological horizon upon which the comparison of the ancient pagans and the contemporary non-European Others was made possible: it was the grid through which they "spontaneously" appeared similar.

III

THE OTHER
IN THE NINETEENTH
CENTURY

The chief difference between the man of archaic and traditional societies and the man of the modern societies with their strong imprint of Judaeo-Christianity, lies in the fact that the former feels himself indissolubly connected with the Cosmos and the cosmic rhythms, whereas the latter insists that he is connected only with History.

Mircea Eliade

It is a question, practically, of relationship. We *must* get back into relation, vivid and nourishing relation to the cosmos and the universe.

D. H. Lawrence

A science of the "human" is not possible, Foucault argues, not because man is qualitatively different from everything else in the cosmos, but because he is precisely the *same* as everything else.

Hayden White

In the cosmography of the sixteenth century, it was *Christianity* which *came between* the European and the non-European Other. Anthropology did not exist; there was, rather, demonology, and it was upon this horizon that the Other took on his specific meaning. In the Enlightenment it was *ignorance* that came between the European and the Other. Anthropology did not exist; there was rather the negativity of a psychology of error and an epistemology of all the forms and causes of untruth; and it was upon this horizon that the Other assumed his significance. In the nineteenth century, finally, it was *time*, geological time, evolutionary time, that came between the European and the non-European Other: "anthropology" ceased being the contestation of demonically grounded ways of life; "anthropology" ceased being the negativity of a *contrast*[1] of ignorance and knowledge; "anthropology" became, finally, the positive and positivist form of a *comparison* between past and present. In the nineteenth century, the non-European Other—as does the "animal"—ceased being the unstable form of a contestation of Western man and now, thoroughly domesticated, became, instead, compared to him. As the epistemological status and significance of the animal undergoes a profound transformation with Darwin's *Origin of the Species* (1859), so, analogously, does the status and significance of the non-European Other in Tylor's *Primitive Culture* (1871). From the moment that "God is dead"—in Feuerbach's rather than Nietzsche's sense—from the moment that, as Foucault says, "philosophy became anthropology" and Western man sought to recognize himself in a natural plentitude, the non-European alien Other lost his power of negativity in order to become—as the animal—between the determinism of nature and the reason of Western man, the positive form of evolution. Nineteenth-century "biology" and "anthropology" are disciplines made possible by the order of a fundamental kinship. They are *theories of kinship*.

WILLIAM PETTY'S SCALE OF CREATURES

Foucault begins *The Order of Things* by noting that in one of his writings, Borges quotes a "certain Chinese encyclopedia" in which it is written that "animals are divided into: a) belonging to the Emperor, b) embalmed, c) tamed, d) suckling pigs, e) sirens, f) fabulous, g) stray dogs, h) included in the present classification, i) frenzied, j) innumerable, k) drawn with a very fine camel hair brush, l) et cetera, m) having just broken the water pitcher, n) that from a long way off look like flies" (Foucault 1970:xv).

This passage affords us a glimpse into a perplexing arena regarding classification: the "similarity" or "difference" of observables is not itself an observable. The "similarity" the "resemblance," the "contrast," and the "difference" between things is not given as a further thing; that two contents of perception are similar or dissimilar, that they resemble or contrast each other, is not given as a third content. Classification is constructive, creative.

If for a moment we confine ourselves to living forms, then it is true to say that classification by the natural system gives us a number of groups which themselves can be collected into larger groups. . . . For example, *man himself is so ob-*

78

*viously a mammal and so close to the great apes and gib-
bons. . . .* (Cain 1954:27, emphasis mine)

The adjacency of science to perception, of our science to our perception, is not without its historicity as Merleau-Ponty (1962) and,
more recently, Donald Lowe (1982) have shown.

The great silent divisions upholding our modern culture that
produce the context of the obvious, the spontaneous certainty of
the conspicuous, the invisible laws of visible difference, have not
always been so arranged, organized and deployed. The story of the
propinquity of things is not as uninterrupted and continuous as
our recently constituted positive sciences with the retrospective
historicizing they authorize and support, would have us believe.

In the second half of the seventeenth century, William Petty, in
addition to his numerous other writings from anatomy to econom-
ics, undertook to arrange in order all animate beings. He terms his
work the "scale of creatures." He makes two adjacent scales, the
Greater Scale having God at the top and—after innumerable "holy
angels, created intelligences, and subtle material beings,"—man at
the bottom. The Lesser Scale, "the Scale of Animals," has man at
the top and the "smallest and simplest animal that man can discern" at the bottom (Petty 1927:21). One of the main problems he
encounters in this enterprise of order is establishing *what comes
next after man*:

> As to the description of the Lesser Scale (whereof man is the
> top and the smallest maggot the bottom) we say as follows: 1)
> Man being the first or top of this Scale, the question is what
> animal shall be next! Unto which question, because no certain
> answer can be given, we shall substitute probable hypotheses
> instead of them, being contented to be confuted or excelled by
> any who shall propound what is more probable, symmetrical
> and congruous, than what we shall at present offer. . . . I
> therefore propound an elephant for the next creature in dig-
> nity to a man, not because of his great strength (which is equal
> to the strength of man assisted by levers and wheels) but rather
> because of his wonderful dexterity arising from the various
> and multiform use and application of his proboscis, which in
> many cases equals, and in some exceeds those of a man's hand.
> 2) I give him the second place for his memory and understand-
> ing, which I have heard extend to the greatest use of the lan-

guage of those men with whom he converses, being the faculty not so eminent in any other animal. Moreover, since longevity, or living till 80 or 90 years of age, doth accompany the dexterity, memory and intellect above-mentioned, it seems to me that the said qualifications, together with his great strength for execution, doth give him a fair pretense to the next place in the Scale after man. 3) In the opinion of most men, the ape or rather the gorilla (which is the largest and most man-like species of apes) should claim the second place unto which we have preferred the elephant, first because his shape is far nearer to that of man, than any other animal's is, and for that his actions as they have been recorded by those who pretend to know them do in many points resemble those of a man. Nevertheless, since it is true that an elephant can understand the language better than a gorilla, and that the *mens* of an elephant doth come nearer the *mens* of a man, although the shape of a gorilla comes nearer the shape of a man, I shall choose to give preference unto the elephant. Speech is more peculiar unto and copious in a man than in any other animal, and consequently we might, in this respect, give the second place to parrots, or that species of them, in which the formation of particular sounds and the imitation of man's speech is most conspicuous. Nor is an ape so considerable to me for imitating the external and visible motions of the parts and organs of a man as speaking birds are for imitating, by a sort of reason and internal sense, the motion of the hidden and unseen instruments of speech, which are the muscle of the lungs and larynx. But it is plain that although parrots do pronounce words, that they do it but as sounds and not like men, as the signs of things, actions and notions; consequently, this faculty of speaking birds extending only to sounds and not to the conception of the mind, I think it not sufficient for degrading the elephant from the second place in the Scale, and serves only to give the parrot a pretense to contest with the ape for precedency. (Petty 1927:26–28).

To a mind already long armed with nineteenth-century biology, Petty's classification appears at its worst as comically ludicrous, at its euphemistic best as highly "prescientific." The very possibility of such an arrangement seems wholly nonsensical, indeed the, we might say, necessity of its appearance as satirical nonsense is a constitutive reflection of the deeply sedimented authority of the nineteenth-century science of biology, as it is of all the nineteenth-century positive sciences and the history they authorize. Petty's arrangement of creatures is, however, neither more nor less "scientific" than that arrangement generated by the nineteenth century; it is merely guided by different values and visibilities and governed by a different epistemological network and system of classification.

There are two elements standing in the relation of tension to each other that propels Petty's thought. The one is the Scale itself, the tabular space of classification, the other is the problem of the form of resemblance and arrangement: to bring together in order those animate beings which most resemble each other. The scale of Creatures is an already constituted, stratified, immobile, ordered space at one end of which, as limit and parameter, stands "man," and at the other end, again as limit and parameter, "the smallest and simplest animal that man can discern." The space of the Scale is not generated by the arranging one after another of the animate creatures, but is already there as the *common space* making juxtaposition and evaluation of appropriateness possible. For Petty, the ordered space of the Scale is not at all problematic, and calls forth no question as to its constitution or origin. It is obviously not one of magnitude, for though at one end of the Scale we have the "smallest and simplest animal," man, at the other end, is certainly not the largest. After determining what comes second to man, the method of differentiation and classification of creatures becomes relatively unproblematic for Petty, i.e., they will be arranged according to their likeness of shape and size and visible appearance:

We have hitherto discoursed whether the elephant, gorilla, parrot, or bee shall have the second place in the Scale, and we have given it in respect of shape to the gorilla, in respect of sound to the parrot, in respect of memory and understanding language to the elephant, but in respect of the spirituality and power to the poor bee. But we shall hereafter more confine ourselves to rank and martial the creatures in the Scale by their shape and visible appearance, rather than by the objects of other senses, or internal operations of the soul, not

81

omitting the difference in the said objects of other senses than that of sight. (Petty 1927:30).

In the vicinity of man, Petty's problem of classification is somewhat analogous to that of a museum coordinator faced with a roomful of statues, paintings, jewelries, manuscripts, miniatures and pottery who must devise a plan of arrangement for them. Shall they be arranged according to color, the light ones on one side gradually shading into the darker ones? Or, rather, according to size, the largest followed by the next largest and so on to the smallest? Or perhaps by what they represent, men here, women there, god's there, animals there? Perhaps chronology should govern order, the most ancient here, the most recent there? The space of the Scale of Creatures is already there, like the museum room—an immobile place upon which creatures will emerge and submit to being differentiated and arranged appropriately according to an autonomous principle of classification brought to that space. In relation to the principle of classification, the space itself stands in universal indifference.

In terms of examining the changing ground of questioning, in addressing the question of what questions are able to be asked, it would seem that in the seventeenth century and, generally speaking, in the Enlightenment as a whole, Order is in no way linked to Origin (Foucault 1972)—problems of order are not at all experienced in the vicinity of problems origin (Lowe 1982). Petty is able to ask, "Man being the first on top of this Scale, the question is what animal shall be next?" In the nineteenth century, the epistemological network alters; one is no longer able to ask this question, the adverbs and adjectives have been slightly altered and one is only able to ask, "Man being the end of the scale, the question is, what came before?" In the nineteenth century, the space of classification, which we may more accurately term the "time of classification," is generated by the very juxtaposition of the creatures. Darwin says,

> Naturalists try to arrange the species, genra, and families in each class, on what is called the Natural System. But what is meant by this system? Some authors look at it merely as a scheme for arranging together those living objects which are most alike, and for separating those which are most unlike. . . . The ingenuity and utility of this system are indisputable . . .

but, Darwin thinks, the rules of the Natural System themselves, as well as long-standing and seemingly unresolvable difficulties, cannot be explained except

on the view that the Natural System is founded on descent with modification—that the characters, which naturalists consider as showing true affinity between any two or more species, are those which have been inherited from common parents, *all true classification being genealogical*—that community of descent is the hidden bond which naturalists have been unconsciously seeking, and not some unknown plan of creation, or the enunciation of general propositions. (Darwin 1962:23)

It is more like our museum coordinator is watching a blob of clay in its raw amorphous state, then awhile later when it takes on the vague outlines of an embrionic appearance, then again when the definite contours of the statue are crystallizing. The space of classification itself has undergone a fundamental rupture and transformation, the transformation of a simultaneous space into a linear time. It is in the region of this profound transformation that "anthropology" first emerges. For the nineteenth century, the age of Historicism, the principle of classification is the principle of historical genealogy. The space of classification becomes identical with the time of genealogical causation. Darwin says that classification "must be strictly genealogical in order to be natural." Darwin does not contest Genesis; he uses it as the principle of classification; the Scale of Creatures is collapsed and superimposed upon the Origin of Creatures, of species, and the problem of classification becomes the problem of specification.

Petty also engages in the problem of differentiating men:

First that of man itself there seems to be several species, to say nothing of giants and pygmies. For of these sorts of men, I venture to say nothing, but that 'tis very possible there may be races and generations of such . . . as we see vast differences in the magnitude of several other animals which bear the same name—as between the Irish wolfdog and the bullonian tumbler . . . so the difference in bulk and weight between a man of seven foot high and him of four foot is near as five to one. And what difference is between the bulk of the one man and another, seems to me to be also in their memories, wits,

83

judgements, and withall in their external senses; some being able to see, others to hear, and others to smell five times as far as other individuals in the same species. . . . Besides those differences between man and man, there be others more considerable, that is, between the Guiny Negroes and the Middle Europeans; and of Negroes between those of Guiny and those who live about the Cape of Good Hope, which last are the most beastlike of all the sorts of men with whom our travelers are well acquainted. I say that the Europeans do not only differ from the afore mentioned Africans in color, which is as much as white differs from black, but also in their hair which differs as much as straight line differs from a circle; but they differ also in the shape of their noses, lips, and cheekbones, as also in the very outline of their faces and the mold of their skulls. They differ also in their natural manners, and in the internal qualities of their minds. . . . The next observation is that men themselves, even of the same nation, are distinguishable from each other by their resemblance, faint or strong, which most men have to some brute or other. Which resemblance the Italians call Carricature, for who hath not seen the spirit of a hawk in some men of bright, clear eyes with high adunc noses. . . . (Petty 1927:30–32)

Petty makes use of two very different methods of differentiation here, one aligned with the ordering principle of the knowledge of the Enlightenment, the other closer to the Renaissance. One is the Lockean notion of primary and secondary qualities: the difference in the size of the races of men being a difference in primary quality; the differences in hair texture, skin color, and internal qualities of mind being differences in secondary qualities. The other Renaissance-aligned method is that of analogical reference. In the Enlightenment the nature of difference is determined on the horizon of nature. For Petty, man is differentiated on the background of nature, and nature is primarily primary qualities and secondarily secondary qualities. There would come a time, at the dawn of the nineteenth century, when the horizon of man's difference would change to that of History: when the Guiny Negroes would differ from Europeans not fundamentally by primary and secondary qualities—not by their size, the color of their skin, their hair texture, or even "their natural manners and the internal qualities of their minds"—but rather fundamentally in the *time in history* in which they lived, i.e., the primitive past, "prehistory." All those earlier phenomenological qualities—hair, color, mind—would no longer make reference to themselves and their difference; they would now become semiological qualities, they would become signs, signs of *a deeper difference,* and only a *new kind* of semiology would be capable of making these signs speak, of scientifically determining their meaning and truth. Behold the new discipline of difference:

> In the reports of crimes which appear daily in the newspapers of our civilized land, such phrases often occur as "savage fury," "barbarous cruelty." These words have come to mean in common talk such behavior as is most wild, rough, and cruel. No doubt the life of the less-civilized people of the world, the savages and barbarians, is more wild, rough, and cruel than ours is on the whole, *but the difference between us and them does not lie altogether in this.* As the foregoing chapters have proved, savage and barbarous tribes often more or less fairly *represent stages of culture through which our own ancestors passed long ago,* and their customs and laws often explained to us, in ways we should otherwise have hardly guessed, the sense and reason of our own. (Tylor 1913:388, emphasis mine)

For Petty, difference is natural difference, *difference is natural,* difference is understood in relation to nature; for Tylor, as for Comte, difference is historical difference, *difference is not natural,* difference is understood truly only in relation to "history"; difference, as with Darwin, is "geneaological." These Others that the travelers tell us about, they are not so much different from as they are similar to Europeans in that they re-present stages that the Europeans have long since progressed beyond in the ever-expanding space of "history." Indeed, the radical explosion of "historical space" in the nineteenth century, the expansion we have come to term "anthropology," "geology," and "evolution," makes possible a wholly new theoretical organization of the difference of the Other.

"Man being the first on top of this Scale, the question is what animal shall be next? Unto which question, because no certain answer can be given, we shall substitute probable hypotheses . . ." (Petty 1927:26). As we have seen, Petty cannot in principle decide whether the elephant, ape, parrot, or bee shall be next. There is an insurmountable and essential ambiguity here. "No certain answer can be given." Why can no certain answer be given? The form of knowledge Petty displays here is *resemblance* (Foucault 1970), and what are witnessing with Petty is a late recrudescence, a gray dying ember catching a breath of air and glowing red one last time before its final darkness. In terms of the form of knowledge, Petty, in many respects, partakes of the Renaissance. We are closer to Cusanus and Paracelsus than to Descartes and Hobbes. Resemblance is what makes knowledge possible, and speech will be recognized as knowledge only if it displays its commitment to following the forms of resemblance:

> Up to the end of the sixteenth century, resemblance played a constructive role in the knowledge of Western culture. It was resemblance that largely guided exegesis and the interpretation of texts; it was resemblance that organized the play of symbols, made possible knowledge of things visible and invisible, and controlled the art of representing them. The universe was folded in upon itself; the earth echoing the sky, faces seeing themselves reflected in the stars, and plants holding within their stems the secrets that were of use to man. . . . How, at the end of the sixteenth century, and even in the early seventeenth century was similitude conceived? How did it organize the figures of knowledge? And if the things that resembled one another were indeed infinite in number, can one, at least, establish the forms according to which they might resemble one another? (Foucault 1972:17)

Foucault goes on to establish four such forms: convenientia (convenience), aemulation (emulation), analogy, and sympathy. It is analogy that is most at work in Petty's scale and in the problems it raises in the vicinity of man.

> The third form of similitude is *analogy*. . . . In this analogy, convenienta and aemulation are superimposed, like the latter, it makes possible the marvelous confrontation of resemblances across space; but it also speaks, like the former, of adjacencies, of bonds and joints. Its power is immense, for the similitudes of which it treats are not the visible, substantial ones between things themselves: they need only be the more subtle resemblances of relations. Disencumbered thus, it can extend, from a singly given point, to an endless number of re-

86

lationships. For example, the relation of the stars to the sky in which they shine may also be found: between plants and the earth, between living beings and the globe they inhabit, between minerals such as diamonds and the rocks in which they are buried, between skin moles and the body of which they are the secret marks. . . . This reversibility and this polyvalency endow analogy with a universal field of application. Through it, all the figures in the whole universe can be drawn together. There does exist, however, in this space, furrowed in every direction, one particularly privileged point: it is saturated with analogies (all analogies can find one of their necessary terms here), and as they pass through it, their relations may be inverted without losing any of their force. This point is man: he stands in proportion to the heavens, just as he does to animals and plants, and as he does also to the earth, to metals, to stalactites or storms. (Foucault 1970:21)

With this aspect of Petty's thought, we are not yet in the Enlightenment world of identities, difference, and analysis, but linger rather in the Renaissance world of resemblance and the sovereignty of the like. Foucault says that for the Renaissance, language is not what it is because it has meaning; somewhat analogously, for Petty, man is not what he is because he is an animal, nor because he is a speaking animal, nor because he is a rational animal. Man is the form of resemblance, the fulcrum of resemblance. He is capable of resembling anything in the macrocosm and this power of analogy constitutes him *as microcosm*. The configuration in *our* knowledge that we term "man" does not yet exist: *man is not yet anthropological;* man is, rather, microcosmical, capable of resembling in his being any possible segment of the universe. The human being, the human's *being*, is seen *primarily cosmically* as microcosm rather than *primarily anthropologically* as "man." As Foucault says of madness, that not until the nineteenth century was it contained in the form of a pathology, so we might say that not until the nineteenth century is the human contained within the form of an anthropology. In the Renaissance, the difference of the non-European Other is cosmically strange; he makes manifest the otherness of the world. In the nineteenth and twentieth century, after the humanization of sensibility, the difference of the Other becomes anthropologically strange; he makes manifest first "man's past" in

87

the evolutionary anthropological perspective, and then "cultural difference," and "cultural relativity" in the antievolutionary anthropological perspective.

"The next observation is that men themselves, even of the same nation, are distinguishable from each other by their resemblance (faint or strong) which most men have to some brute or other . . . and it is also observed that such men in which those resemblances and carricaturas are strong and plain, do partake in some measure with the same brutes as to their internal qualities of physiognomy or rather metoscopy. (Petty 1927:31)

For the Renaissance, man is essentially the ambiguous power of analogy, who, in his prolific instability, does not allow a "certain answer" as to what animal comes next in the Scale of Creatures. He has not, indeed, he could not, yet allow himself to submit to being "fixed in his species"; he has no species: he is essentially unstable—"uncertain" and not "clear and distinct" as Descartes would find and denounce him; he is a volatile, perpetually writhing complex of analogies, a continual coming and going of resemblances; he is a constant, lightning-like communication with the four quarters of the universe.

GEOLOGY, EVOLUTION, AND ANTHROPOLOGY

The leading idea which is present in all our researches, and which accompanies every fresh observation, the sound which to the ear of the student of nature seems continually echoed from every part of her works is—Time! Time! Time! (Scrope 1858:208)[2]

In the nineteenth century a strange new formation began to become visible on the outermost distances of the European horizon. At first it appeared but a small rise on the horizon, as a wave, that, instead of cresting and breaking as usual, allowing calm and the horizon to be restored, began rather to slowly ascend and grow, to rise up more and more, higher and higher, and disturbingly to form itself on the hitherto flat horizon of the Enlightenment, until, acquiring more and more momentum and velocity, one day it finally towered up over the European horizon lifting that very horizon itself up, up and back over itself like a vast and gigantic tidal wave, and in the midst of this loss of horizon, in the center of this sheer cultural vertigo, there occurred the sudden, epistemologically violent eruption of time into space. There occurred Lyell's *Principles of Geology* (1830), Darwin's *Origin of the Species* (1859), and Tylor's *Primitive Culture* (1871):[3] Geology . . . Evolution . . . Anthropology: each was, I believe, a distinct extension, a distinct yet interdependent individualization of the same fundamental epistemological network. The concept of the discipline of "geology," the concepts of "evolution" and "anthropology" were, from this perspective, various "statements," "expressions," made possible by the same "deep grammar," the same paradigm; and their respective founders, their "authors," were more or less aware of this. In 1844 Darwin wrote,

> I always feel as if my books came half out of Lyell's brain, and that I never acknowledge this sufficiently; nor do I know how I can without saying so in so many words—for I have always thought that the great merit of the *Principles* was that it altered the whole tone of one's mind, and therefore that, when seeing a thing never seen by Lyell, one yet saw it partially through his eyes. (Darwin 1903:117)

How close to Kuhn's notion of 'paradigm' that last sentence sounds! E. B. Tylor wrote in his *Anthropology* (1881):

> Thus geology establishes a principle which lies at the very foundation of anthropology. Until of late, when it used to be reckoned by chronologists that the earth and man were less than 6000 years old, the science of geology could hardly exist, there being no room for its long processes of building up the strata containing the remains of its vast successions of plants, and animals. These are now accounted for by the theory that geological time extends over millions of years. It is true that man reaches back comparatively little way into this immense lapse of time. Yet his first appearance on earth goes back to an age compared with which the ancients, as we call them, are but moderns. (Tylor 1913:33)[4]

For Tylor, geology authorized and made possible the concept of "prehistory," which was absolutely necessary for the constitution of modern "anthropology." Geological "time" gave anthropology

the space it needed to account for the slow, progressive evolutionary rise of the human condition from savagedom to civilization.
Much of Tylor's "anthropology" is governed by a kind of geological
vision, a kind of displaced geological metaphor. It is metaphori-
cally geological, if I may, following Turbayne's *Myth of Metaphor*
(1962), use Gilbert Ryle's definition of a "category mistake" as a
definition of metaphor, i.e., metaphor is the creative presentation
of the facts belonging to one category in the idiom appropriate to
another. Tylor's "anthropology," in so far as it is metaphorical geology, creates the similarity rather than simply formulating some
similarity already existing. "The institutions of man are as dis-
tinctly stratified as the earth on which he lives. They succeed each
other in a series substantially uniform over the globe, independent
of what seems the comparatively superficial differences of race and
language, but shaped by similar human nature acting through suc-
cessively changed conditions in savage, barbaric, and civilized life"
(Tylor 1888:245). Finally, Tylor's successor at Oxford, Robert R.
Marrett, wrote:

> Anthropology is the child of Darwin. Darwinism makes it pos-
> sible. Reject the Darwinian point of view, and you reject an-
> thropology also . . . for anthropology stands or falls with the
> working hypothesis derived from Darwin, of a fundamental
> kinship and continuity amid change between all the forms of
> human life. (Marrett 1914:8)

This geologic-time-revolution in the nineteenth century was perhaps as significant in the Western tradition as the earlier Copernican revolution.

> If our ideas about the past are now no longer restricted within
> the time-barrier of earlier ages, this is due above all to the
> patience, industry, and originality of those men who between
> 1750 and 1850 created a new and vastly extended time-scale.
> During this time . . . men lived with uncertainties as pro-
> found, and dilemmas as agonizing, as those provoked earlier
> by Copernicus' reforms in astronomy. . . . In some ways the
> situation was even more difficult. (Toulmin and Goodfield
> 1965:141)

And Lyell himself compared the radical extension of the "time-
scale" necessary for the construction of "geology" with the earlier
revolution in the "space-scale"

90

It was not until Descartes assumed the indefinite extent of the celestial spaces, and removed the supposed boundaries of the universe, that a just opinion began to be entertained as to the relative distances of heavenly bodies; and until we habituate ourselves to contemplate the possibility of an indefinite lapse of age . . . we shall be in danger of forming most erroneous and partial views of Geology. (quoted in Toulmin and Good-field 1965:170)

At the formation of geology the *duration* of time was seen *as comparable* to the dimension of space and the revolution in the dimensions of stellar space was experienced as being analogous to the revolution in terrestrial time, i.e., the formation of "geologic time." Lyell's geology was, in a very real sense, a tremendous expansion of the concrete human imagination. He sought to "broaden man's horizon respecting the earth's duration" and experienced, after his foremost difficulty of liberating the science of geology from the Mosaic record, from "mosaic geology," the difficulty of overcoming the human imagination and its tendency to "take alarm at the immensity of time required" it by geology. With geology, "time" became almost limitless, and the vastness of "geological time" was as alarming and as disturbingly heavy to the human imagination as the immensity of "astronomical space." Philosophers have debated since the Greeks whether the universe was eternal or not, but this, however, was entirely different from the historical formation of the concrete geological imagination. (Eternity is not the same as when time is limitless, as infinity is not the same as when space is endless. Hegel, Blake, many have taught us this.) The Western philosophical mind has known "the eternal" for a long time; the introduction of the concrete vastness of geological time—connected, one might suspect, with nineteenth century "historicism"—is a quite recent event and one that was a necessary precondition for the formation of "anthropology."

In the space opened up by "geological time" Darwin found the room he needed to construct "evolution." "As natural selection acts solely by accumulating slight, successive variations, it can produce no great or sudden modifications; it can act only by short and slow steps" (Darwin 1962:361). For Darwin, only infinitesimally small and continuous variations could bring about gross and visible differences; and because the difference in the species was not primordial but the daughter of time, it was only after he found the theoretical field of vision opened up by "geological time" that he could adequately construct "evolution." "Biologists had, of-course, a virtually unlimited amount of time in the past with which to make gross differences the cumulative and continuous results of minute differences" (Nisbet 1969:175). The intellectual interdependency of nineteenth century geology and biology is here, I believe, most manifestly shown: biological evolution presupposes geological time.

In regard to "man," Darwinian "evolution" represented in one important sense the transcendence of Enlightenment Order and the return of Renaissance Resemblance, i.e., the transcendence of the central Enlightenment commitment to and perception of a relatively stable Order, via the return to the primary Renaissance experience of a relatively unstable Resemblance, as in its famous perception of the macrocosm and microcosm.

> At the beginning of the seventeenth century . . . thought ceases to move in the element of resemblance. Similitude is no longer the form of knowledge but rather the occasion of error, the danger to which one exposes oneself when one does not examine the obscure region of confusions. "It is a frequent habit," says Descartes, in the first line of his *Regulae*, "when we discover several resemblances between two things, to attribute to both equally, even on points in which they are in reality different, that which we have recognized to be true of only one of them." The Cartesian critique of resemblance . . . is classical thought excluding resemblance as the fundamental experience and primary form of knowledge, denouncing it as a confused mixture that must be analyzed in terms of identity, difference, measurement and order. (Foucault 1970:51–52)

Philosophically, the Darwinian concept of evolution was based on a transcendence of the confines of that more or less Cartesian epistemology and scientific order, which was founded upon the suspicion and exclusion of resemblance, by means of the authoritative return of the Renaissance perception of resemblances: of both the "visible" relations of resemblance and the "invisible" resemblance of relation, i.e., the analogy. Darwinian evolution was thus founded upon the *organic analogy*.

Evolution constituted itself in the transcendence of the hitherto almost universally acknowledged absolute distinction between "rational man" and "mechanical nature." Nineteenth-century "evolution," as incompatible with "mechanical nature" as it was with "rational man," represented in one of its deepest senses a recognition of the possibility of an order common to reason and animality, such that

> in the aftermath of evolution-theory any absolute opposition between human reason and animal instinct begins to appear a decided exaggeration. The essential point is not that human nature is less rational than our forefathers believed; it is, rather, that many animals already display in embryo form those modes of behavior which are quoted to prove the rationality of man. (Toulmin and Goodfield 1965:243)

Evolution reasserted man's animality by rediscovering man's analogy to the cosmos. As a result of this, "man," for modernity, comes not directly *out of nature*, but rather directly *out of evolution*. Because of the Darwinian concept of evolution the modern definition of "man" is now, once again, a "rational animal."

DIFFERENCE ACQUIRES HISTORICITY

> No doubt the life of the less civilized peoples of the world, the savages and barbarians, is more wild, rough and cruel than ours is on the whole, but the difference between us and them does not lie altogether in this. As the foregoing chapters have proved, savage and barbarous tribes often more or less fairly represent stages of culture through which our own ancestors passed long ago, and their customs and laws often explain to us in ways we should otherwise have hardly guessed, the sense and reason of our own. (Tylor 1913:388)

In the age of historicism, anthropology consitituted a historicizing of the different, as the works of Morgan and Tylor clearly make manifest. Nineteenth-century anthropology was grounded upon a double transformation: first it transformed difference into *historical* difference, and then it transformed history into evolution (progressive evolution). As Lyell reconstructed the surface of geography into the temporal depth of geology (geology is the temporalization, the historization of geography: "The stony rocks are not primeval, but the daughters of time," Linnaeus), and as Darwin

93

reconstructed the great smooth surface of eighteenth-century classificatory natural history into the depth of biological evolution, so
Tylor reconstructed the surface of non-European differences into
the depth of a historical evolution. He made difference historical
and history evolutionary. The Other now made manifest not a
stratification of behavior, as in Enlightenment "ignorance" and
"superstition," but a stratification of time. The Other was no longer
a representation of ignorance; he was now a representation of historical evolution. *Beyond* Europe was henceforth *before* Europe.
Nineteenth-century anthropology, from this perspective, existed then
as the axis whereby differences residing in geographical space were
turned and turned until they became differences residing in developmental historical time, i.e., the axis whereby the simultaneity
of geographical space was transformed into the successive linearity of historical evolutionary time. It represented the rearrange-
ment and transformation of a *comparative table of differences into
a geneaological scale of development.*

Nineteenth-century anthropology was interested in the origins
of man in early times, in "life then," and, in order to study that,
it undertook to make "life now," as the non-European Other, represent, re-present, "life then." It transformed the non-European
Other into being the document of predocumented history and the
living peoples of the world were arranged, classified, and built up
into a stratified schema as though they were the historical peoples
of the world. The "world" also, which hitherto had been everywhere contemporary with itself, became partitioned off into different times, different time epochs, and much of it was seen as a
living museum. Societies that were other than our own were actually primitive expressions of our own society. These Others, these
petrified peoples, re-presented our ancient ancestors, i.e., they presented us with vivid contemporary memories of our ancient long
gone past. Anthropology transformed the Other into being a concrete memory of the past. In this, like the museum principle, it
attempted to overcome time by extending our memory by means
of a spatial juxtaposition. It's like a new system of mnemonics. In
nineteenth century anthropology the non-European Other was seen,
by means of a technique precisely isomorphic with its geological
counterpart, *as a fossil.* Anthropology fossilized difference; it saw
difference as fossilization. The non-European Other was a petrified
European, and his difference was merely a petrified sameness.

Tylor doesn't say the "tribes" *are* at the same stages our ancestors went through: they *represent* those stages. Anthropological discourse isn't concerned with what the tribes are "in themselves" but with what they represent. It's concerned with our ancestors: the savage tribes make our ancestors present again. One tribe represents the next stage and so on. The living people can represent the dead ones in a kind of global congress whose purpose is to reveal to us our origins. It's as though Tylor saw the whole world as a huge museum-drama: on stage one, in the Amazon, for instance, we can see act one. Simultaneously, on stage two, in New Guinea, we can see act two, etc. The people of the world act out the story of *our* history, and the only audience who can understand the play is, of-course, "us." We have the benefit of hindsight: we know how the story ends, we *are* how the story ends. In this sense Tylor assumes there is a purpose in the world and that purpose is "us."

The politics of knowledge implicit in Tylor's constitution of anthropology seem to dictate that "man" comes to know his own situation by "placing himself" in a parallel yet less advanced situation and from there traces his own development. The "sense and reason" of "our" culture cannot be known through the direct study *of* our culture: the "sense and reason" of culture can be known only through its development, not through the culture itself. This constitutes the justification of the new science and institution of anthropology: for without anthropology how could we ever hope to understand ourselves?

"Their customs and laws explain to us, in ways we should otherwise have hardly guessed, the sense and reason of our own." Our customs and laws have no "sense and reason." They are senseless, meaningless: they are *in need of* explanation, they are *in need of anthropology*. Further, regarding these savage and barbarous tribes, we're not trying to explain them; we're trying to explain ourselves. "Their customs and laws" are outside the core of the sentence, peripheral to it—as in substance, practice and philosophy so also in grammar, the Other is peripheral. At most, they provide the occasion for Tylor's assertion. The statement implies that "savage tribes" are merely the occasion for anthropology: the real subject of anthropology is our own culture and its real object is to understand ourselves. Tylor, along with all of nineteenth-century anthropology *wants* the savage tribes to be like out ancestors; he assumes his audience wants it too. He wants to believe it because he assumes that to know ourselves we must know our ancestors; we

95

must know the past in order to know the present. Above all else, Tylor wants self-knowledge. (Anthropological discourse to a large extent takes up its abode and inhabits this particular comparative project and historicist version of "self-knowledge." How do we know ourselves? By knowing our ancestors. How do we know our ancestors? By knowing the savage tribes. How do we know them? By comparing them to us. But how do we know us? And so the circle starts again.)

"The We of anthropology . . . remains an exclusive We, one that leaves its Other outside on all levels of theorizing . . ." (Fabian 1983:157). In terms of the politics and grammar of its universe of discourse and at its very inception as an institution unconsciously geared to re-produce Western society, anthropological discourse speaks *of* the Other but never *to* the Other. Conversationally and dialogically Tylor's first assumption deals with the nature of his audience: he clearly does not see the "less civilized people of the world" *as part of his audience;* he is not speaking to the people he is speaking *about.* Tylor uses the terms "us" and "them" and then equates "them" with the "savages and barbarians." To do this he must assume and *thereby help produce and establish the situation* that members of his audience will be able to identify themselves as part of the collectivity labelled "us." This particular concept of "us" also includes Tylor himself within this collectivity. Supposedly the reader-collaborater will know automatically that he is one of the "us" rather than one of "them." Nineteenth-century anthropological discourse secures, identifies, and institutionalizes itself by systematically excluding the possibility that a person it considers to be "savage" (i.e., one of "them") might read (and collaborate with) this statement and "misclassify" himself as an "us." Thus anthropological discourse assumes that either all "savages" naturally identify and consider themselves to be "savages" or that all savages are "illiterate," or will not have access to anthropological discourse and therefore will not be faced with this choice of identity.

Nineteenth-century anthropology took its sustenance from and saw itself as the life-long preoccupation with attempting to minutely, methodically, and scientifically answer the question, which like a great impersonal abstract womb, gave it birth: *Why are there such vast differences in development?* And how have these differences in development come about? It multitudinous answers consisted, in large part, of pointing to myriad and wondrous instances of "evolution." What made this "scientifically respectable" project and preoccupation possible, however, was the prior setting up and organization of a system of relationships between the different societies present on earth: the vast differences of mankind were fundamentally presumed to be differences *of development*.

Tylor saw difference as ontologically unreal; it was not a primary existent but a secondary illusion, i.e., difference—in the human as in the organic sphere—is always the result of the modifications on the same. If the non-European Others's difference was truly comprehended, i.e., if it was anthropologically understood (if we recognize the validity of the establishment of the "science of anthropology") it would vaporize and vanish. If we but look anthropologically at these alien Others who initially appear different we will be able, finally, to see their truth, which is that they are the same as we used to be. Their continuity with us, their essential sameness with us—we who observe and study them—is both affirmed and denied, and it was in the dialectics of this oscillating affirmation and denial that nineteenth-century anthropology took up its precarious abode. They are not the same as we are, hence they're different. But they are the same as we used to be, hence they're similar. When we study them we study, not ourselves, but our past. And when we study them we study, not them, but our past. This makes clear, I think, the Other's essential prehistorical mode of being, which is his essential historical function and dimension, and in this sense nineteenth-century evolutionary anthropology may be seen as essentially a species of the more generic nineteenth-century category of "History," in a similar sense in which we saw eighteenth-century Enlightenment "anthropology" as a species of the philosophy of error.

The last years of the eighteenth century are broken by a discontinuity similar to that which destroyed Renaissance thought at the beginning of the seventeenth century. . . . The Classical order distributed across a permanent space the non-quantitative identities and differences that separated and united things: it was this order that held sovereign sway . . . over men's discourse, the table of natural beings, and the exchange of wealth. From the nineteenth century, history was to deploy, in a temporal series, the analogies that connect distinct organic structures to one another. This same History will also, progressively, impose its laws on the analysis of production, the analysis of organically structured beings, and, lastly, on the analysis of linguistic groups. History *gives place* to analogical organic structures, just as Order opened the way to *successive* identities and differences. Obviously, History in this sense *is not to be understood as the compilation of factual successions* or sequences as they may have occurred; *it is the fundamental mode of being of empiricities*, upon the basis of which they are affirmed, posited, arranged, and distributed in the space of knowledge for the use of such disciplines or sciences as may arise. . . . *History, from the nineteenth century, defines the birthplace if the empirical*, that from which, prior to all established chronology, it derives its own being. (Foucault 1970:217, emphasis mine)

What authorized Tylor's project of establishing and legitimating a "science of anthropology"? He assumed, as we have said, that difference was fundamentally unreal, was not a primeval, indelible, and persisting dimension of the earth's people, but rather that the difference between our society and those non-Euopean societies was the result of progress (as the geologist's rocks are not primeval but the daughters of Time). The nineteenth century's anthropological perception of difference was systematically governed by its peculiar valorization of time, i.e., its belief that civilization progresses, developing through stages from the primitive to the advanced. It is here, in this belief in progress, that we may locate one of the central supports of its edifice.

The alien Other is not fundamentally pagan, savage, and demonic from a Christian frame of reference, nor fundamentally ignorant and superstitious from an Enlightenment frame of reference; rather the Other is now *fundamentally primitive* from a progress and evolution frame of reference. The concept of progress was what made possible the experience of the *Other-as-primitive*, of the Other-as-fossil. The deeply sedimented concept of progress in Western sensibilities was what made *our experience of the non-European's alien difference an experience of his "primitiveness,"* of his backwardness (both in terms of the Enlightenment's order of "knowledge" and in terms of the nineteenth century's order of "evolutionary development.")[5] Without our whole sensibilities being formed and informed by the concept of progress, being organized and ordered by the historical a priori of progress, we would have never, in encountering and confronting difference, experienced

98

"primitiveness," experienced our advance over their backwardness, our linear growth over their linear fossilization. The resource
of "progress" authorizes the transformation of the "different" into
the "primitive." If the rather deeply sedimented, institutionalized
belief in "progress" disappeared, the "primitive" would vanish.

In *Time and the Other* Fabian remarks, "A discourse employing
terms such as primitive, savage (but also tribal, traditional, Third
World, or whatever euphemism is current) does not think, or observe, or critically study, the "primitive"; it thinks, observes, studies *in terms of* the primitive. *Primitive* being essentially a temporal
concept, is a category, not an object, of Western thought" (Fabian
1983:17). Wittgenstein says somewhere that naming presupposes,
rather than makes possible, language (language is not the result of
induction, the mathematical result of inductive naming). "The
primitive" was not the reflex name given to that which was immediately present to the senses. The very identification of and
naming of the non-European Other as "primitive," as "primitive
mentality," as "primitive culture," presupposed a theory (language) of rational progress, of progress in and by reason (Enlightenment) and/or progress in and by history (nineteenth century).
The very possibility of the conception of "primitive" presupposed
the prior commitment to a conception of progress. It was not the
factual "discovery" of "primitive peoples"—"primitive people" are
not the sort of thing that can be "discovered": "primitives" are
made, not found—in the sixteenth through the eighteenth centuries that slowly, inductively, taught the European that his condition was that of "an advanced civilization," that forced him finally
to recognize that it was that great impersonal force "progress" that
was continually operating behind his back which caused him to
be where he was. Rather, it was only through this Eurocentric construction of and commitment to the concept of "progress" and its
discriminating employment (its employment in discrimination) that
"primitive peoples" came into being. The "factual" existence of
"primitive peoples"—"primitive peoples" are not a fact, but an
interpretation—did not slowly, gradually, yet inevitable reveal to
the European the reality of progress; rather the invention and in-
stitutionalization of progress in the mode of anthropological discourse created "primitive peoples." Progress produces primitives;
primitives do not prove progress. Primitives *are* progress, the dark,
velvety, necessary reverse underside of the concept. Fabian ad-
dresses this concept in its contemporary function.

The term *primitive* . . . is the key term of a temporalizing discourse. . . . What is gained or changed if primitive is used in quotation marks, or preceded by *so called* and similar disclaimers? Perhaps these modifiers signal the label-character of the term, its conventional, classificatory function in a technical vocabulary. But disclaimers may be indexical rather than referential. In that case they point to the position of the primitive in anthropological discourse. Who calls the primitive *so called?* Anthropologists. (Fabian 1983:176)

THE SCALE OF DEVELOPMENT

The admiral came forward with uncovered head and extended one hand, while the old king saluted him by a stately flourish of his weapon. The next moment they stood side by side, these two extremes of the social scale—the polished splendid Frenchman, and the poor tatooed savage. They were both tall and noble looking men; but in other respects how strikingly contrasted! At what an immeasureable distance, thought I, are these two beings removed from each other! In the one is shown the result of long centuries of progressive refinement, which have gradually converted the mere creature into the semblance of all that is elevated and grand; while the other, after the lapse of the same period, has not advanced one step in the career of improvement. "Yet after all" quoth I to myself, "insensible as he is to a thousand wants, and removed from harrassing cares, may not the savage he the happier man of the two?" (Melville 1974:33)

In the nineteenth century most of the discourse about the alienness of the non-European Other was a discourse about development. How can discourse on difference be transformed into a discourse on development? How can difference be seen as manifesting development? Why does every speech about difference find itself willy-nilly and in spite of itself being transformed into a speech about development: the nature and laws of development, of progress, of evolution, the causes of development, of historical development, the value or good or evil of development, of civilization, etc. etc. How can difference make reference to development? How can difference be made to represent development, to show, to manifest development? Melville, in this extremely Tylor-like passage of

Typee, experienced difference as a function of distance; not distance in space, nor distance in time directly, but distance on a scale of development. Difference was a function of distance on a scale of development. Hence, as with Tylor, difference was real in that there are different locations on the scale, but it was also unreal in that it is ever the same scale; the scale is not different, it is homogenous and everywhere identical with itself. Difference, as a function of distance, was subsumed under the concept of change, developmental change. Difference was thereby both superficially preserved and fundamentally destroyed: difference was tamed and domesticated into serving as a manifestation of social change, and change, likewise, was domesticated and changed into being change-of-development. Difference then could be seen as being a manifestation of the continuity and order of social change. Nineteenth-century anthropological discourse would seem to rest on the rather geometrical assumption that different peoples are parallel peoples at different stages within the same homogenous historical time. "Human history" looks something like figure 3.1

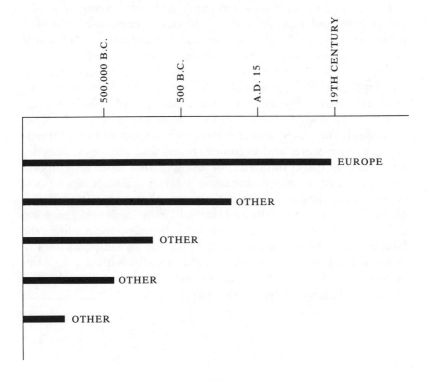

In the sense of this anthropology of history, past and present could coexist at the same time: "It does not affect the main result that different tribes and nations on the same continent, and even of the same linguistic family, are in different conditions at the same time, the condition of each being the material fact, the time being immaterial" (Morgan 1877:13). In nineteenth-century anthropology, *past and present became contemporary with each other*, because different peoples passed through these fixed stages of development at different velocities.

> Comte recognized, of-course, that all people had not passed through the same stages *simultaneously*. The fact that they had not is what made the use of the Comparative Method possible. Comte handled the problem of cultural differences by asserting that special racial, climatic, and political factors had operated—apparently fortuitously—to vary the *speed* of progress in different societies, but not the basic *course* of progress. (Bock 1956:33)

The nineteenth century's temporal scale of development was everywhere contemporary with itself; it was everywhere simultaneous with itself. Yet the occupants, once arranged on it on the various "stages," were seen as coming before and after one another, as earlier and later than one another, like the linear and serial museum arrangement of rock, stone ax, flint knife, iron knife, bow and arrow, rifle, cannon, and atomic missile. One could go "backwards" and "forwards" in time on this temporal scale of development. One could move, travel, with respect to time. Time is stopped, as it were, and becomes spatial and immobile in order that one may travel through it or along it. Difference as temporal distance, however, only makes sense in terms of a scale of temporal development that is not itself temporal, that is not itself developing, but that is immobile and static, like the yardstick. Temporal distance, in short, is possible only if it is based on the analogy, the false analogy, to spatial distance: "There is no temporal field of vision corresponding to a spatial field of vision—it's a false analogy—since events which are earlier and later than one another, by definition do not coexist" (Gale 1967:154).

TIME TRAVEL

In 1800, at the beginning of the century, Degérando teaches us in *The Observation of Savage Peoples,* "The philosophical traveller, sailing to the ends of the earth, is in fact travelling in time; he is exploring the past; every step he makes is the passage of an age" (Degérando 1969:63). And then again at the end of the century: "Going up that river was like traveling back to the earliest beginnings of the world, when vegetation rioted on the earth, and the big trees were kings" (Conrad 1950:102). So Marlow, the narrator of Conrad's darkly profound *Heart of Darkness* (1890) describes his voyage up the Congo river into Africa. How available that type of metaphor now is; how easy it comes to us now. Kuhn says somewhere that our education comes between us and the past, and I think he is correct. The lens of contemporary consciousness retrospectively bends and refracts the light of the past, and familiarity, over-familiarity, breeds blindness more than contempt. Going up the Congo river "was like traveling back into the earliest beginnings of the world." In the later part of the nineteenth century, for the first time, time travel becomes possible. No Columbus nor Magellan, no Hakluyt explorer, no Bougainville nor Diderot, no Crusoe nor Swift, no traveler either actual or imaginary in the Enlightenment or in the Renaissance could have experienced his voyage as a voyage in time, as a traveling back through time or, indeed, as a traveling forward through time, as does Marlow's fictional contemporary, "The Time Traveller" in H. G. Wells' *The Time Machine* (1895). Nineteenth-century anthropology is in many respects precisely a time machine. "Systematic study of "primitive" tribes began first in the hope of utilizing them as a kind of time-machine, as a peep into our own historic past, as providing closer evidence about the early links in the great Series" (Gellner 1964:18). In terms of historiography, of course "going back," empathizing with, reconstructing and scrutinizing the past, past ages, was possible along the stepping stones of documents, of the historically documented. (History, one might say, is dependent on writing, is a function of writing.) But literal time travel ("imaginatively literal," imaginatively sensible), physical time travel, the direct experience of oneself being bodily taken back through time was not hitherto conceivable. That path in the forest of the imagination did not exist until the peculiar configuration brought about by nineteenth-century knowledge made it possible. One had always been able to imagine what the past was like. What's new is that now one is able to imagine not what the past was like, nor even oneself being back in the past, as in living in the past (as in *A Connecticut Yankee in King Arthur's Court*); rather, one is able to *imagine oneself traveling back into the past*, into past epochs. This is not a suspension of time, as in Eliade's *Cosmos and History* (1949), but a traveling through time, through the medium of time, a traveling with respect to time.

> "Clearly," the time traveler proceeded, "any real body must have extension in *four* directions. . . . There are really four dimensions, three which we call the three planes of Space, and a fourth, Time. . . . There is no difference between Time and any of the dimensions of Space except that our consciousness moves along it. . . . Scientific people," proceeded the Time Traveler, "know very well that Time is only a kind of Space." (Wells 1961:194)

Time is a kind of space: in the nineteenth century time became a medium capable of supporting travel; it was seen as capable of supporting a material adventure. In the age of positivism time was materialized; it took on its own viscosity. For Marlow journeying up the African Congo, as for the anthropologist, to look into this primitive area was to look back in time and to travel into this primitive space was the equivalent of traveling back in time. For nineteenth-century evolutionary anthropology going beyond Europe now took on the meaning of going back in time. Going beyond is going back. (Hence also the "transcendence" of science fiction, so different from fantasy and fairy tale, now took on its peculiar and relatively stable form—for it too, every going beyond was a going forward, a going ahead, a time travel.) As Lyell's geology, following Linnaeus, was the first to massively and intrinsically include the element of time *within* the very definition of geography (the earth's surface is not primeval but the daughter of time), and as Darwin's biology, following Lamark, was the first to intrinsically include the element of time immanently within the very definition of the species, so nineteenth-century anthropology was the first to splice the dimension of time immanently inside the experience and definition of the otherness of the non-European Other, inside the definition of traveling beyond Europe, and inside the

definition of European "civilization" or "culture." Human difference is not primordial but the daughter of evolutionary time. For
nineteenth-century evolutionary anthropology, time, in short, for
the first time becomes an environment, becomes space-time. In the
nineteenth century time acquires a "dimension."

NATURE OR CULTURE

When the inhabitants of some sequestered island first descry
the "big canoe" of the European rolling through the waters
towards their shores, they rush down to the beach in crowds,
and with open arms stand ready to embrace the strangers. Fatal embrace! They fold into their bosoms the vipers whose sting
is destined to poison all their joys; and the instinctive feeling
of love within their breasts is soon converted into the bitterest
hate. . . . How often is the term "savage" incorrectly applied! None really deserving of it were ever yet discovered by
voyagers or by travellers. They have discovered heathens and
barbarians, whom by horrible cruelties they have exasperated
into savages. It may be asserted without fear of contradiction,
that in all the cases of outrage committed by Polynesians, Europeans have at some time or other been the aggressors. (Melville 1974:30)

Herman Melville's *Typee* (1844) offers us, I think, a densely complex and classic portrait of the early nineteenth century's conception of the non-European Other, especially on the more aesthetic,
elegiac, and pastoral rather than on the directly theoretical and
scientific end of the spectrum of that experience; and on this account it is not unlike Defoe's *Robinson Crusoe* and its relation to
the Enlightenment. It is a work of fierce integrity that insists on
the beauty of these beings while simultaneously acknowledging their
unintelligibility. It crystalizes and brings together into a clear unity
the major emotional and intellectual paths along which Europeans
experienced and made sense of non-Europeans. *Typee* is the "dra-
matized" account of Melville's life among the Typees—he lived with
them for a little over a month—a "tribe of cannibals" on one of
the Marquesan islands in the Pacific. On first coming to port on
the island of Nukuheva, Melville remarks of the natives, who are
not the wild Typees, but their neighbors,

105

Its inhabitants have become somewhat corrupt, owing to their recent commerce with the Europeans; but so far as regards their peculiar customs, and general mode of life, they retain their original primitive character, remaining very nearly in the same state of nature in which they were first beheld by the white man. The hostile clans residing in the more remote section of the island, the Typees, very seldom holding any communication with foreigners, are in every respect unchanged from their earliest known condition. (Melville 1974:17)

With regard to the non-European Polynesians, the central visibles on Melville's horizon of concern are that (a) they are in the state of nature, and (b) contact with white European civilization corrupts them.[6] These two relatively clear and distinct forms are common to much of mid-nineteenth century Europe's experience of the alien Other. Alfred Russell Wallace, co-founder with Darwin of the Origin of Species, draws similar forms out of his experiences in the Amazon river valley in the late 1840s. "Looking back over my four years wandering in the Amazon valley, there seems to me to be three great features which especially impressed me, and which fully equalled or even surpassed my expectations of them . . ."; after registering his wonder at the virgin forests and the infinite variety of bird and insect species, Wallace goes on,

The third and most unexpected sensation of surprise and delight was my first meeting and living with a man in the state of nature—with absolute uncontaminated savages! This was on the Uaupes river, and the surprise of it was that I did not in the least expect to be so surprised. I had already been two years in the country always among Indians of many tribes; but these were all what were called tame Indians, they wore at least trousers and shirt; they had been nominally converted to Christianity, and they were under the government of the nearest authorities. . . . But these true wild Indians of the Uaupes were at once seen to be something totally different. . . . In every detail they were original and self-sustaining, as are the wild animals of the forest, absolutely independent of civilization, and who could and did live their own lives in their own way, as they had done for countless generations before America was discovered. I could not have believed that there would be so much difference in the aspect of the same people in their native state and when living under European civilization. (Wallace 1905:288)

If, as we have attempted to show, Tylor and Morgan "historicize" difference, so, we might say, Melville and Wallace here "romanticize" difference—and that is in no way intended as a pejorative judgment; it is one historically available way to treat difference. With Wallace, as with Melville, contact corrupts, contact infects the pristine state of nature of the Other, and the state of nature of the Other reveals, above all, the nature of civilization. For Melville, the very existence of the Typees represents a profound questioning, a radical interrogation of our Hobbesean way of life:

> During the time I lived among the Typees, no one was ever put upon his trial for any offence against the public. To all appearance there was no courts of law or equity. . . . And yet everything went on in the valley with a harmony and smoothness unparalleled, I will venture to assert in the most select, refined, and pious associations of mortals in Christendom. How are we to explain this enigma? These islanders were heathens! savages! ay, cannibals! and how came they without the aid of established law, to exhibit, in so eminent a degree, that social order which is the greatest blessing and highest pride of the social state. It may reasonably be inquired, how were these people governed? How were their passions controlled in their everyday actions? It must have been by an inherent principle of honesty and charity towards each other . . . It is to this indwelling, this universally diffused perception of what is *just* and *noble* that the integrity of the Marquesans in their intercourse with each other is to be attributed. (Melville 1974:190)

There follows a Hobbesean list of all the measures they *don't take* to insure their security and property. Their beauty questions our ugliness, their muscle our flab, their happiness our misery. A profound incoherence and a deeply obsessive contradiction grounds, haunts, and animates Melville's narrative, driving it forward: How is it that such an uncivilized people can be so civilized? How can such uncivilized savages be the most civilized people he has ever seen?

White European civilization constitutes with regard to the natural Polynesians an instantaneous contagious disease, a pollution, a syphilis: as concrete physical intercourse with Europeans has brought about, most dramatically, syphilis, so cultural intercourse, commerce, communication, has brought about cultural syphilis. When the "sun" of civilization dawns on the virgin forest of the Other, instead of nourishing him, it chars and blackens him. European "development" degenerates them. Bastian put it thus in 1881 in a political treatise arguing for the acknowledgment of ethnology as a scientific discipline and proposing to establish ethnographic museums as its primary research institutions: "For us, primitive societies (Naturvölker) are ephemeral, i.e., as regards our knowledge of, and our relations with, them, in fact, inasmuch as they exist for us at all. *At the very instant they become known to us they are doomed* (Quoted in Fabian 1983:122). Melville, in his own way, also comes to the realization, the tragic "ethnographic insight" that, in despite of his honest and whole-hearted sympathy with and admiration of the Typees and their mode of life, he too is in complicity with this European disease: for in this "ethnographic situation" the observer alters what he observes by the very act of observing it. He further realizes that the publication, the communication, of *Typee* in that European category known as "the book," will undoubtedly hasten and itself thereby contribute to the alteration and European corruption of the Typees. With this so-called "romantization of difference" we may mark the first *ecological* awareness of difference.

The non-European Other is experienced-as-susceptible-to-being-corrupted (like the "child"). It is not, however, one culture corrupting another culture (like "adults"), for neither Melville's Polynesians, nor Wallace's Amazons, nor Alexander von Humboldt's Amer-Indians (1811 and 1848) are experienced on the horizon of the not yet extant anthropological concept of culture. They are, rather, in a "state of nature": they are not different from European culture because *they have* their *own* different culture, they are different from European culture because *they are* the same as nature (nature as surrounding "environment" and nature as "authentic human nature").

TIME OR NATURE

We penetrated deeper and deeper into the heart of darkness. . . . We were wanderers on a prehistoric earth, on an earth that wore the aspect of an unknown planet. We could have fancied ourselves the first men taking possession of an accursed inheritance. . . . But suddenly as we struggled round a bend, there would be a glimpse of peaked grass roofs, a burst of yells, a whirl of black limbs, a mass of hands clapping, of feet stamping, of bodies swaying. . . . The steamer toiled along. . . . The prehistoric man was cursing us, praying to us, welcoming us—who could tell? We were cut off from the comprehension of our surroundings. . . . We could not understand because we were too far and could not remember because we were traveling in the night of first ages, of those ages that are gone, leaving hardly a sign,—and no memories. . . . It was unearthly, and the men were—No, they were not inhuman. Well, you know, that was the worst of it—this suspicion of their not being inhuman. . . . They howled and leaped . . . but what thrilled you was just the thought of their humanity—like yours—the thought of your remote kinship . . . a dim suspicion of there being a meaning in it which you—you so remote from the night of first ages—could comprehend. (Conrad 1950:105)

So Marlow narrates in 1890. Contrast this with another voice in 1890:

Life each day became better. I understand the Maori tongue well enough by now. . . . My neighbors . . . look upon me as one of them. My body almost constantly nude, no longer suffers from the sun. Civilization is falling from me little by little. I am beginning to think simply, to feel only very little hatred for my neighbor—rather to love him. All the joys—animal and human—of a free life are mine. I have escaped everything that is artificial, conventional, customary. I am entering into the truth, into nature. (Gauguin 1970:40)

What a difference in formulating difference! What a difference in the way Conrad with the thrill of horror and Gaugin with nostalgia for the truth of simplicity integrate the Other into our world.

For Conrad the non-European Other makes essential reference to a dark prehistoric past, whereas for Gaugin, as for Melville, the Other makes essential reference to a harmonous and indefinitely present nature.

For both, however, the "primitive" is *our guide*, as he has been since Cooper's Leatherstocking novels, our guide to nature, or our guide to the prehistoric past. He shows us; he makes manifest "nature"; he makes manifest "our past."

That the principle rules of transformation of nineteenth-century evolutionary anthropological discourse have already become deeply sedimented in practically all speech about the non-European Other, may be clearly seen in parts of D. H. Lawrence's reading of Melville's work in his classic *Studies in Classic American Literature* (1920).

> Melville went back to the oldest of all the oceans, to the Pacific. . . . The Maoris, the Tongans, the Marquesans, the Fijians, the Polynesians: holy God, how long have they been turning over in the same sleep. . . . The scientists say the South Sea Islanders belong to the Stone Age. It seems absurd to class people according to their implements. And yet there is something in it. The heart of the Pacific seems like a vast vacuum, in which, mirage-like, continues the life of myriads of ages back. It is a phantom persistence of human beings who should have died, by our chronology, in the Stone Ages. It is a phantom, illusion-like trick of reality. Back, back. . . . (Lawrence 1960:144)

Melville, however, like Gaugin, like Wallace, like Humboldt, does not experience himself as traveling *back in time*, back to past ages, but rather as *stepping deeper into nature;* and what Stanley Cavell has said of Thoreau's Walden experiment holds equally well for Melville and Gaugin's quest: they call, not for the return *to* nature entailing some kind of retrograde, temporal route, but, rather, for the return *of* nature, as of the repressed. The Polynesian inhabitants of the Pacific, Lawrence tells us, should have *died by our chronology*. Perhaps we might say our chronology kills them. Our anthropologically informed and organized Western chronology makes these Others long dead, makes them representatives of the long-ago, the dead, the buried and lost. "The absence of the Other from our Time has been his presence in our discourse—as an object and victim" (Fabian 1983:xi). *Our* chronology, our ordering and valorization of time, our experience, conception, and coding of "history" kills them. It transforms them into the "living dead." The field of our modern chronology and the grid of our modern history, organized by the magnetic lines of "anthropology," the concept of "geological time," and an evolutionary principle of genealogical classification, makes the non-European Other a phantom, an historical echo, the ghost of our ancestors. In this context nineteenth-century anthropology in the double movement of its quest to historicize the present and to resurrect the past may be seen, precisely, as a necrology practiced on the living.

CONCLUSION

We have only to speak of an object to think that we are being objective. But, because we chose it the first place, the object reveals more about us than we do about it.

Gaston Bachelard

For the other remains to be discovered. . . . And just as the discovery of the other knows several degrees . . . so we can indeed live our lives without ever achieving a full discovery of the other. . . . Each of us must begin it over again in turn; the previous experiments do not relieve us of our responsibility.

Tzvetan Todorov

In the late nineteenth and early twentieth centuries, another enigmatic and radical reformulation of the non-European Other occurs. Not until the twentieth century does *"culture"* emerge; not until the twentieth century does "culture" become part, a decisive and almost inescapable part, of our world.[1] With regard to the strange and alien Other, difference is now, for the first time, *seen as cultural difference*, as *cultural diversity. Culture accounts for difference*, rather than "evolution," "progress," evolutionary development through fixed stages of progressive civilization, as in the nineteenth century; rather than the various possible modalities of "ignorance" and "superstition" as with the Enlightenment; and rather than the demonical and infernal as with the Renaissance. Our contemporary experience of "culture" as the universal ground and horizon of difference marks a rupture with the nineteenth-century concept of culture:

> Tylor's presumed status as founder of American cultural anthropology is predicated on the assumption that the 'culture' he wrote about in *Primitive Culture* is essentially the same as that studied by modern cultural anthropologists. . . . Tylor's

113

actual usage of the term "culture" lacked a number of the features commonly associated with the modern anthropological concept: historicity, integration, behavioral determinism, relativity, and—most symptomatically—plurality. For though it still is spoken of as "the science of culture," modern cultural anthropology might be more accurately characterized as the "science of cultures." . . . Whatever impulse Tylor may have had to embrace the idea of cultural plurality and relativity was constrained by his evolutionary commitment. (Stocking 1987:302–303)

The experience of differene as cultural difference is contemporary with our historical time. It constitutes the historic element within which we move, within *our* experience of difference, of the Other. The "totalizing concept of culture" is shared by all the twentieth century's different schools of anthropology (Fabian 1983:156). The emergence of the concept of "culture" has made possible the democratization of difference (perhaps, in one sense, "culture" *is* the radical democratization of difference). The twentieth-century concept of "culture" has rescued the non-European Other from the depths of the past and prehistory and reasserted him in the present; he is, once again, contemporary with us. Twentieth-century "culture" was a concept forged in the teeth of "evolution," in a struggle to the death with "evolution" and the hierarchic schema implicit in it. Twentieth-century "culture" has killed "evolution," and mortally wounded "historicism." The formation of anthropological "culture" is an interiorization of "time" (and "history"), and of "value," for now, instead of the evolutionary-historicist perspective whereby all difference was to be seen on the universal ordering horizon of temporal historical evolution, anthropology now sees the conception of temporal, historical evolution against the broader, universal horizon of "culture." "History" is interiorized into "culture."

TRAVEL AND CULTURE

Some complete their demoralization by extensive travel, and lose whatever shreds of religion remained to them. Everyday they see a new religion, new customs, new rites (La Bruyere).

Peter Berger, in a passage highly representative of the conventional interpretation of the history of the growth of our modern anthropological awareness, provides a concise formulation that sees in travel, concrete ethnographical travel (induction), the central cause of modernity's slow and gradual growth into a cosmopolitan, mature anthropological awareness of cultural relativism:

> The unprecedented rate of geographical and social mobility in modern society means that one becomes exposed to an unprecented variety of ways of looking at the world. The insights into other cultures that one might gather by travel are brought into one's own living room through the mass media. . . . No doubt this sophistication is commonly only superficial and does not extend to any real grappling with alternate ways of life. Nevertheless, the immensely broadened possibility of travel, in person and through the imagination, implies at least potentially the awareness that one's own culture, including its basic values, is relative in space and time. (Berger 1963:49)

According to the conventional interpretation of the history of anthropology, then, concrete travel and exploration has made an awareness of other and different cultures possible. Travel, anthropological travel (i.e., ethnography), has profoundly educated us; it is, in fact, the defining characteristic of our modern sophisticated consciousness. Exposure to difference makes us different. In fact, exposure to difference is, if I read Berger correctly, *the criteria of our difference* both from our premodern forefathers and from the "primitive cultures" we have finally become aware of. (This is a rather quantitative concept of travel and exposure; it seems to forget that the nontraveler is exposed to the traveler's difference, or in ethnological terms, the field observer is himself a field of observation, a "tribe" for the tribe, the "observer.")

Ethnography is now established as *the* foundation of any possible "anthropology," the empirical *practice* and *institution* without which any *theory* would be impossible (Fabian 1983). How is modern ethnographic travel possible? We are addressing here not the *content* of modern travel, but the *concept* of modern travel. What are the conditions for the historical appearance of the possibility of travel, i.e., of travel-as-a-method-of-acquiring-knowledge? What are the conditions of the conceivability of travel?

Travel does not produce an awareness of difference; rather, travel presupposes an awareness of difference (as we have seen with "primitives" and progress, i.e., that "primitives" presuppose rather than prove the existence of progress). Travel assumes rather than discovers difference. Awareness of difference is not the analytic result of travel—imaginary travel, travel literature—but the precondition of the possibility of the concept of travel. "Exotic otherness may be not so much the result as the prerequisite of anthropological inquiry" (Fabian 1983:121).

Travel, as it comes to lodge itself in the heart of the modern anthropological awareness, is not a mere random gazing but rather an intentional undertaking, a methodology systematically used in acquiring knowledge of "man." What is the secret presupposed ideal of adequate knowledge that authorizes and allows one to see in travel a powerful method for systematically acquiring knowledge of man? How is it possible to see geographical movement (mobility) as intellectual method? To think is to travel. To travel is to see—travel is essentially a way of seeing, a mode of seeing; it is grounded in the eye, in our visual capacity. The traveler is Argus-eyed; there are no blind travelers or explorers in either physical or imaginary voyages. To think, therefore, is to see, to observe:

The modernity of this world can be seen in the fact that the version of adequate knowledge which it produces is a version which treats observing as knowing. . . . Movement becomes method in a world in which observation is the paradigm of knowing and when learning requires being present and having visual access. Travel becomes educational in such a world. . . . The connection between movement and education is grounded in an ideal of knowing as experiencing. . . . To say this then, is to say that the world which supports travel as a method for creating intelligible knowledge is a metaphor for the world which science creates as its ideal. It is a world which assumes the identity of knowing and observing, which sees the impediment of being stationary, which equates real change with the movement of commanding a view, and with exposure to the experience of the new. Movement educates by emancipating a person from inexperience (from innocence), and this is possible only in a world where being in one place is seen as ignorance." (McHugh, Raffel, Foss, Blum 1974:150)

Again, Berger, "The immensely broadened possibility of travel . . . implies at least potentially the awareness that one's culture, including its basic values, is relative in space and time." Travel implies the "democratic" awareness that one's own culture is relative. Such a view presupposes that there is such a thing as *one's own culture*, as one's *owned* culture, the culture that one owns privately (a rather capitalistic definition of culture). It presupposes that one can *have* a culture, i.e., that "culture" is of such a nature (like capital) as to support being possessed. Our relation to culture is fundamentally in the mode of *having*. There is an objectlike character to culture such that we possess our culture rather than, say, are possessed by it, or inhere in it. This view assumes that human consciousness is in essence an a-cultural tabula rasa and comes to be aware of a culture (as an objective object) rather than the view that consciousness is culture (or that culture is like the grammar of consciousness).

One's own culture is relative. Culture is one of the things that can be relative—like what else? opinions? views? values? languages? *Culture is* and *culture is relative.* What we term "anthropology" is that region which opened up in the field of knowledge in virtue of the recognition of *the being* of culture, by means of, or on the occasion of, the recognition of the existence of other cultures. In the introduction to a reader on symbolic anthropology we hear: "Fundamental to the study of symbolic anthropology is the concern with how people formulate their reality, We must, if we are to understand this . . . examine *their culture*, not *our theories*" (Dolgin et al. 1977:34). Against this view one might say "examining their culture" *is* our theory. In terms of its self-identity as a discipline anthropology thereby contains within itself the project, however remote, of a global and exhaustive ordering, interpretation, and explanation of the world and all the items in the world in terms of "culture." One's culture is one-among-many. There is then no such thing as a universal culture, no primordial monolithic culture—culture is not such that to be uniformly homogenous is essential to its nature. It is, moreover, not a unity-in-multiplicity, but a unity amidst a multiplicity of unities. Culture, by definition, by anthropological definition, is *cultures;* and cultures, by anthropological definition, are *relative.* Perhaps one might say ethnographical travel and anthropological "culture" *transforms difference into relativity,* a democratic relativity, a perpetually tolerant relativity. As the resource of "progress" authorized the transformation of the "different" into the "primitive," so the resource of anthropological "culture" authorizes the transformation of "difference" into "relativity." We may mark here a paradoxical redomestication and annihilation of difference, for if all cultures are democratically relative, then in this respect, in this deep respect, none are different. It is in this region that Castaneda's works, in one sense, mark an unquiet on the horizon of contemporary anthropology: *are* they anthropology or *are* they fiction . . . anthropology is beginning more and more to disbelieve its own story line, to question its self-identity. Anthropology is able less and less to chew on its own thought categories (Duerr 1978). Paul Riesman in a review of Castaneda's works sees this same phenomena:

> When we study "other cultures" this way, we assume in advance that "understanding" means "explanation" in terms with which we are already familiar from our own experience and knowledge of what the world is like. To put it another way, anthropological understanding is a way of making the world feel safer, a way of extending the edge of order so that we can comfortably say that people are fundamentally the same everywhere and that "cultural differences" are merely something like different mental images of the same basic reality. I used to think, in fact, that one of anthropology's great humanistic contributions to our civilization was the notion of a basic humanity common to all mankind—a humanity that was only differently emphasized or differently expressed in different cultures. This idea has been repeatedly used to argue that no race is superior or inferior to any other, and that different cultural accomplishments are not the result of different genetic endowments. Although I have used this argument myself, I believe now that it has been an ineffective and perhaps even irrelevant one for the fight against racism, and that it has actually held back the progress of anthropology because it has almost invariably led us, as Dorothy Lee has shown . . . to confuse equality with sameness and inequality with difference. Paradoxically, then, the belief that all people are human leads to a *disrespect* for other people as they are, for in the back of our minds we are saying: They could be just as good as we if they tried, or if they adopted different cultural patterns. . . . The belief that all people are human has not saved Western anthropologists from feeling superior to the people they study and write about. . . . (Riesman 1972:7)

118

CONCLUSION

All phenomena, authropologically speaking, make reference to
the relative being of culture—except the phenomena of anthropology, i.e., except the phenomena of seeing-phenomena-as-making-
reference-to-the-relative-being-of-culture, *that* is somehow exempt;
that is somehow not cultural, not relative, but of the nature of things
and of the order of truth. A sociology of sociology, one might say,
makes sense, whereas an anthropology of anthropology doesn't.
There is a structural inability to perceive anthropology as an activity that is part of what it studies. In this sense a protective *lack*
of reflection is what makes possible the discipline: anthropology
is thus essentially grounded on a structural incapacity to account
for itself. It has, as Gödel showed Russell's formal mathematics to
have, an essential and intrinsic structural incompleteness as its very
foundation.

Ethnographic travel is a looking at relativity from within an un-
acknowledged absolutest framework, rather than a direct experience (nonvisual, nonvisualizable) of the relativity of frameworks.
Travel transforms the encounter with otherness into a qualitatively homogenous medium through which one encounters heter-
ogeneous cultures. The ethnographic traveler is one who sees himself as essentially independent and hence thereby experiences all
others as essentially dependent. Ethnographic travel as a universal
medium, as a universal method for acquiring knowledge, is neither
essentially contained in nor essentially an aspect of *our* culture,
and it thereby gives access to (produces) essentially nonuniversal
particular cultures. Because travel is conceived of as a universal
methodology it produces a perspective that is not itself culture-
bound.

Again, Berger, ". . . that one's own culture, including its basic
values, is relative in space and time." Against this one might say
culture doesn't "include" or "contain" its basic values; it *is* its basic values. Further, one of our culture's "basic values" is that *it* is
relative in space and time. This concretely spatializing mode of
comprehension must needs assume that "culture" is *in* space and
time the way an object is in a box. To concretely *see*, to concretely
visualize "cultures" as being shut up in time and space necessarily
presupposes that the anthropological observer is above all these
boxes seeing the relativity of what's contained in each culture box.
To generate a prison theory of cultural relativity, of subjects shut
up in their boxes, necessarily presupposes a free warden, i.e., an
absolute spectator—which, of course, is a self-contradiction to the

119

whole relativity theory. Merleau-Ponty has formulated most concisely perhaps the strongest analytic challenge to this way of seeing:

> The concept of history [or culture] in its most profound sense does not shut the thinking subject up in a point of space and time; he can seem to be thus contained only to a way of thinking which is itself capable of going outside all time and place in order to see him in his time and place. Now it is precisely this presumption to absolute thought which is discredited by the historical sense. . . . "You believe you think for all times and all men," the sociologist [or anthropologist] says to the philosopher, "and by that very belief you only express the preconceptions or pretentions of your culture." That is true, but it is no less true of the dogmatic sociologist than it is of the philosopher. *Where does he speak from,* the sociologist [or anthropologist] who speaks in this way? The sociologist can only form this idea of an historical time [or "culture"] which allegedly contains philosophers as a box contains an object by placing himself outside history [culture] in turn and claiming the privileged position of an absolute spectator. (Merleau-Ponty 1964:109)

From the anthropological perspective, one of the basic values of our culture is that it and its basic values are relative, i.e., that it is one culture among many essentially unrelated cultures. These multiple self-contained unities exist in a relation of indifferent exteriority one to the other (except for "diffusion"). Our culture *knows* that it is one-among-many, knows that it is relative, and further, it *values* this knowledge (this knowledge is one of its basic values), i.e., it locates its own superiority (knowledge) in this knowledge of its relativity, as it likewise locates inferiority (ignorance) in ignorance of this relativity:

> A: Have you seen the Tahitian whom Bougainville took on board and brought back here? B: Yes. He was called Aotourou. He took the first piece of land he saw for the home of the travellers. Either they had lied to him about the length of the journey, or else he was deceived quite naturally . . . and knew nothing about the real measurement of the earth. . . . The holding of women in common was a custom so well established in his mind that he threw himself on the first European woman he met, and very seriously intended to show her the courtesy of Tahiti. (Diderot 1969:116)

120

The Other becomes *an occasion for seeing the strength of custom.* He manifests, above all, his own imprisonment within culture. We see the logically necessary, relativity, whereas they are governed by the psychologically customary, absoluteness. Anthropology sees how the alien is imprisoned in his culture, his way of life. Bougainville, it will be remembered, was himself, while in Tahiti, able to adjust and participate in their customs. This relationship to difference has constituted our belief in our "superiority" for centuries; as Todorov remarks, Western Europe's

> way of life and its values have spread around the world; as Columbus wished, the colonized people have adopted our customs and have put on clothes. This extraordinary success is chiefly due to one specific feature of Western civilization. . . . European's capacity to understand the other. Cortez affords a splendid example of this . . . [he] slips into the other's skin. . . . Thereby he ensures himself an understanding of other's language and a knowledge of the other's political organization . . . in so doing he has never abandoned his feeling of superiority; *it is even his very capacity to understand the other that confirms him in that feeling.* (Todorov 1984:247, emphasis mine)

A principle characteristic of the Other, then, is that he is incapable of recognizing otherness. In the modern anthropological perception of the alien Other, he is—as Foucault says of the madman—Different only in so far as he is unaware of Difference. The principle characteristic of different cultures, anthropologically conceived, is their inability to recognize difference, i.e., their inability to recognize, as we do, their own relativity. Our knowledge lies in the fact that we recognize, not, as in the Enlightenment, our ignorance, but rather our relativity: our relativity *and* their relativity, whereas their ignorance lies now in their cultural absolutism.

> The simplest observational judgments, the most natural impulses of the will, the rules and customs traditionally passed down—all these are taken by the naive man as absolute. The various expressions of the inner life of man in government, law, and business, in art, morality and learning present themselves as absolute in their origins, their spontaneous growth, and their dominance over convention. Every form of religious devotion, within the boundaries of its sphere of influence, quite

naturally and as a matter of course regards itself as absolute, and every world religion does the same in every conceivable sphere. *Absoluteness is a universal characteristic of the naive way of thinking.* (Troeltsch 1971:133, emphasis mine)

Absoluteness is *the* characteristic defining naive thinking. It is in and through their irrepressible absoluteness that the "primitives" are homologized with the "peasants," with the naive. Absoluteness, belief in the universality and necessity of its thinking, is a universal characteristic of naive thinking. Awareness of relativity, of particularism, then, is a universal characteristic of sophisticated (scientific) thinking. Belief in relativity is a universal characteristic of sophisticated thinking. Sophisticated (scientific) thinking, however, insofar as it sees belief in universality as a universal characteristic of naive thinking is itself immediately capable of knowing universal truths, and it too believes in the truth of these universals—namely, that it is a universal characteristic of naive thinking that it thinks its thinking is universal. But if sophisticated thinking knows this is a universal characteristic then it too thinks itself capable of thinking universal thoughts and is hence not at all different from naive thinking. We do not have any beliefs without believing in them. Stanley Rosen perhaps has best captured the essential indefensibility of any anthropological doctrine of radically and absolutely incompatible "Weltanschauungen" or "cultures":

The sense in which we circumscribe the whole is itself reflected in the different conceptions of the determinate structure of the whole. The *difference* between those conceptions is intelligibility. . . . It is a failure to appreciate the force of this difference which leads some thinkers to a doctrine of radical, and radically incompatible, Weltanschauungen [cultures], that is, of beginnings irrational because indefensible, each distinct from and excluding the others, among which no genuinely philosophical dialogue is possible. This doctrine, which even in its "historicist" form is closely related to the emergence of modern epistemology, results from a common human failure to remember that a refusal or inability on our part to discuss our presuppositions makes them neither secure nor undiscussible. If we can identify our presuppositions and thereby distinguish them from other presuppositions, then there must be a common environment of intelligibility within which this discrimination takes place. We must be able to understand the difference between our presuppositions and those of other thinkers, and the intelligibility of the differences is itself different from any of the presuppositions in question. That is, the intelligibility of the differences is independent of the adoption of any given position. . . . The incompatibility of Weltanschauungen is therefore either intelligible or unintelligible. If it is intelligible, the theory is wrong, since this intelligibility must be shared by all and so be separate from each. . . . If it is unintelligible, then no rational distinction can be made between Weltanschauungen, and it makes no sense to speak of their incompatibility or difference; thus they cannot intelligibly be said to be incompatible, and the theory is again wrong. (Rosen 1969:225)

ETHNOGRAPHY AND CULTURE

"We begin with the supposition that anthropology is based on ethnography. All anthropological writing must draw on reports resulting from some sort of concrete encounter between . . . ethnographers and members of other cultures." (Fabian 1983:88). Because difference is now, prior to any theoretical formulations, democratically experienced as *cultural difference*, the germinal project of ethnography, of participative-observation-in-the-field now lodges itself as the foundation of twentieth century "anthropology." Ethnography, not only as method, or as "data gathering," but as an activity, as field-*work*, as communicative interaction with an Other is regarded as the legitimation of what counts for us as anthropological knowledge. "It should be noted here that culturally different persons who are serious about understanding each other spend long periods of time working out translation problems. A good example is the anthropologist doing field work" (Mackay 1974:184). (This holds also for twentieth-century "ethology," so different from nineteenth-century biology and comparative anatomy; for the Lorenzs, the Goodels, the Fosseys, who are, above all, participant observers in the field, among various animals, and who study animal "behavior," animal "culture." It is more or less within this similar framework that it first becomes valuable and sensible to study animal behavior.) Ethnography as

123

participation and as description, and, in its more sophisticated forms, as translation, only becomes possible when the non-European Other is experienced as before all else culturally different. This pretheoretical legitimizing framework, however, preserves-while-denying the same historical power relations toward the alien Other insofar as "participant observation" is really interested in observing rather than participating; i.e., it is analytically really about observation rather than participation; it is epistemologically committed to the sovereignty of observation and its monologue *about* the Other rather than the democracy of genuine participation and its dialogue *with* the Other:

> Those ritually repetitive confrontations with the Other which we call fieldwork may be but special instances of the general struggle between the West and its Other. A persistant myth shared by imperialists and many (Western) critics of imperialism alike has been that of a single, decisive conquista, occupation, or establishment of colonial power, a myth which has its complement in a similar notion of sudden decolonialization. . . . Both have worked against giving proper theoretical importance to overwhelming evidence for *repeated* acts of oppression. . . . We cannot exclude the possibility, to say the very least, that repetitive enactment of field research by thousands of aspiring and established practitioners of anthropology has been part of a sustained effort to maintain a certain type of relation between the West and its Other. To *maintain* and *renew* these relations has always required coeval recognition of the Other as the object of power and/or knowledge. . . . (Fabian 1983:149)

In a review of a number of books dealing with Indian–White relations, *I Have Spoken: American History Through the Voices of the Indians; The Memoirs of Chief Red Fox; The First Hundred Years of Nino Choise; Geronimo: His Own Story; Bury My Heart at Wounded Knee: An Indian History of the American West;* Peter Farb comes across a profound ethnological paradox:

> The history of Indian–White relations, of course, is multi-colored. . . . All of the books under review are attempts to recover this history. Their common problem is that the red man has not been able to take part in the modern business of writ-

124

ing, editing, and publishing his own history. . . . In all these books whites serve at least as collaborators . . . the whites recognize that they are intruding upon the very history they are attempting to recover. Once a white becomes the collaborator or author of Indian history, he has the responsibility of judging the validity of his source materials. This can be very burdensome. Almost all of the Indian speeches and narratives that have been preserved were delivered in native languages and transcribed by whites who had no linguistic training . . . the white who originally recorded Two Legging's story through an interpreter, "could not have been aware of the close attention the Crows paid to antithesis, parallelism, repetition, hyperbole, soliloquy, rhetorical queries, and symbolic expression." We are thus presented with a problem: the Indian whose story is most valuable because least contaminated by white culture must tell it in his own mode (poetic, repetitious, symbolic, nonsequential, and so on) which makes it unacceptable or incomprehensible to whites. (Farb 1971:36)

Anthropology lives by seeing and interpreting everything as culture-bound . . . everything but itself. Anthropology's participant observer, the field ethnologist, appears on a concrete level to be engaged in intercourse with the "natives," with the non-European Other. Analytically, this intercourse or dialogue is a fantasy, a mask, covering over and hiding his analytic monologue or masturbation. Analytically, to continue the erotic metaphor, he never "loses control." He never loses control over his horizon, his anthropological horizon. He never really doubts the rightness of, and the authority and auspices of anthropology. All the field ethnologist's activity is projected toward one end: internal-comprehension-of-the-alien-culture. What participant-observation-grounded-knowledge (ethnology) necessarily strives for as its absolute goal and limit is simulated *membership* in the alien culture it is seeking to comprehend. It seeks to acquire full knowledge of membership without commitment to membership. (Against this one might say "membership" lies more in commitment rather than in concrete knowledge.) Anthropology's field ethnologist exercises his utmost effort to *become a native* and herein reveals the paradox at the basis of anthropology: if he succeeds he fails and disappears. As Castaneda's works make manifest, if he *becomes a native*, if he submits to that absolute laceration that alone gives him access to the "other world," he can no longer *be an anthropologist*, he can no longer *do* anthropology, for the tiny yet pivotal reason that then "anthropology" does not exist. It ceases to be and ceases to be conceivable. Doing our "anthropology" is not within the parameters of membership, not within the form of life (Wittgenstein 1958), of that alien "culture." The conditions of anthropology's possibility—in all their subterranean depth—are no longer there.

"But what after all are man's truths? . . . they are his irrefutable errors," Nietzsche. And Wittgenstein, "From it seeming to me—or to everyone—to be so, it does not follow that it is so. What we can ask is whether it can make sense to doubt it." The only real dialogues are Socratic in nature; they are the most difficult as well as the most dangerous. The cardinal condition of the Socratic dialogue is the ability to be in ignorance, the ability to actively question and recognize one's own ignorance, the ability to seriously play with the possibility that one is in ignorance. Socrates held to this because he was able to envision, maintain, and sustain the commitment to the indefinitely present possibility that he himself was in ignorance. Aristotle replaced the analytic character of the Socratic dialogue, by preference, with the analytic monologue (Blum 1974). In contrast to the Socratic view of ignorance, Aristotle could interpret wrongdoing (deviance) as voluntary and knowledgeable wickedness only on the prior condition and commitment that he could not doubt the rightness of his position, that he could not conceive nor seriously play with the possibility that he didn't know right from wrong doing, that he himself was in ignorance. Anthropological discourse accounts for the deviance of difference as "cultural" difference by means of an Aristotelean monologue rather than a Socratic dialogue. In this sense it bears a deep structural similarity to modern psychiatric discourse:

> In the serene world of mental illness, modern man no longer communicates with the madman. . . . As for a common language, there is no such thing; or rather, there is no such thing any longer. . . . The language of psychiatry [anthropology], which is a monologue of reason *about* madness [the difference of the Other], has been established only on the basis of that silence. I have not tried to write the history of that language, but rather the archaeology of that silence. (Foucault 1965:260)

126

Both what we contemporarily call "anthropology" and "psychiatry" have been analytic monologues, institutionally secure in their own positions, unable to question their own position, to put its rightness in question. Anthropology has been an extremely subtle and spiritual kind of cognitive imperialism, a power-based monologue, a monologue *about* alien cultures rather than, and in active avoidance of, a dialogue with them in terms of sovereignty, i.e., the untranslatability and irreducibility of one "culture" to the being and language of the other. Anthropology is interested in the Other and at the same time remains altogether alien to the Other; in the best of cases anthropology speaks well *of* the Other, but with very few exceptions, anthropology does not speak *to* the Other and it is as Todorov says (1982) only by speaking *to* the Other—not giving orders but engaging in dialogue—that I can acknowledge him as subject, comparable to what I am myself. The, in Ong's phrase, decay of dialogue (Socratic dialectic dialogue), the atrophy of dialogue, is, thus, the *condition* of our contemporary anthropological discipline. Anthropological "scientific method" *is* the decay of dialogue, the sustained, cultivated, and epistemologically enforced atrophy of dialogue:

> The grammarians's "third person" is opposed to the first and second person as a *nonparticipant in the dialogue.* . . . "What differentiates 'I' from 'you' is first of all the fact of being, in the case of 'I' *internal* to the statement and external to 'you'; but external in a manner that does not suppress the human reality of dialogue". . . . Ethnography addresses a reader. The dialogic Other (. . . the other anthropologist, the scientific community) is marked by the present tense; *pronouns . . . in the third person mark an Other outside the dialogue.* He (or she or it) is not spoken to but posited (predicated) as that which contrasts with the personness of the participants in the dialogue. (Fabian 1983:85)

As psychiatry has been the modern West's monologue about madness and unreason, so anthropology has been the modern West's monologue about "alien cultures." Anthropology never *listened* to the voices of "alien cultures," it never *learned* from them, rather it studied them; in fact studying them, making sense out of them, making a "science" about them, has been the modern *method* of *not* listening, of avoiding listening, to them. The Other's empirical presence as the field and subject matter of anthropological discourse is grounded upon his theoretical absence as interlocutor, as dialogic colleague, as audience (Fabian 1983). In order for modern anthropology to sustain itself, its monologue about alien cultures, those cultures must be kept in analytic silence. The moment that an alien culture is allowed to speak its language, the moment the anthropologist seriously plays with the possibility of the truth and authority of that alien culture, the monologue-based language of anthropology bursts. The whole work, on different levels, of Carlos Casteneda and Mircea Eliade bear witness to this:

> Castaneda, like nearly every member of Western civilization, feels himself to be superior to members of other cultures and in fact to all other entities in the world. But since such feelings conflict with our democratic ideology, he claims that Don Juan is his equal. Don Juan not only sees through this, but also sees that Castaneda's . . . reason for being there in the first place is not to learn something but to collect information for someone else: to add to the corpus of anthropological knowledge. . . . But knowledge of what? . . . Our social sciences generally treat the culture and knowledge of other peoples as forms and structures necessary for human life that those people have developed and imposed upon a reality which we know—or at least our scientists know—better than they do. We can therefore study those forms in relation to "reality" and measure how well or ill they are adapted to it. In their studies of the cultures of other people, even those anthropologists who sincerely love the people they study almost never think that they are *learning something about the way the world really is*. Rather, they conceive of themselves as finding out what other people's *conceptions* of the world are. For the longest time Castaneda, too, thought this way about what Don Juan was telling him. (Riesman 1972:14)

As madness assumes an objective sovereignty with Foucault, so "alien cultures" with these men assumes an objective sovereignty: the Other is "objective," is sovereign, an absolute category existing in, of, and by its own right, and not answerable nor subsumable to the modern West's "deeper categories" of explanations. Morally and legally speaking, as well as philosophically speaking, Neighbors, not Minors and Teachers, not Subjects.

IN CONCLUSION

The man who finds his country sweet is only a raw beginner;
the man for whom each country is as his own is already strong;
but only the man for whom the whole world is as a foreign
country is perfect (Eric Auerbach).

To see the Other as culturally different is no cause for applause
and self-congratulation. To *see difference* as "only" difference or as
"merely" difference is itself an accomplishment rooted for the most
part in the late Enlightenment, when bourgeois good-conscience
became troubled and self-conscious with regard to the non-European Other, and insisted, for the sake of good-conscience, that *the
Other is not-inferior-but-different.* The initial formulation of the non-
European Other as different, then, was grounded upon the bour-
geois-moralistic denial that he is inferior . . . and hence, also, superior.[2] This marks not a moral nor an intellectual victory but rather
a great trivialization of the encounter with the Other; and as, at
this time, madness, in an awesome move, becomes "merely madness," so the non-Europan Other becomes "merely different." To
say then that since we now see the non-European Other democratically as merely having a different culture, as being fundamentally "only" culturally different, we have a more just idea of
her, a less prejudiced and truer idea of her than did the nineteenth
century who saw her on the horizon of historical evolutionary development, the Enlightenment who saw her on the horizon of ignorance, or the Renaissance who saw her on the horizon of the
demonical, would be merely to reaffirm the Eurocentric idea of the
progress of knowledge; i.e., it would be to instantaneously, retro-
actively, and totally transform this work from being an archaeology of the different conceptions of difference into being, once again,
a history of the progress of anthropological knowledge and an affirmation and celebration of the teleology of truth.

NOTES

INTRODUCTION

1. For a definitive critique and deconstruction of this "faith" in reference to science see Kuhn (1970) and Karatheodoris (1978), in reference to philosophy see Wittgenstein (1958) and Husserl (1970), in reference to history see Collingwood (1946) and Foucault (1970), and in reference to sociology see Garfinkel (1970) and Blum (1974).

1. THE OTHER IN THE RENAISSANCE

1. The attempt will be to determine the *savoir* ("knowledge") in Foucault's sense, upon which the *connaissance* ("knowledge") of sixteenth-century cosmography is founded: "By *connaissance* I mean the relation of the subject to the object and the formal rules that govern it. *Savoir* refers to the conditions that are necessary in a particular period for this or that type of object to be given to *connaissance* and for this or that type of enunciation to be formulated." (Foucault 1972:15)

2. Richard Eden (1521–1625), Richard Hakluyt (1552–1616) and Samual Purchas (1575–1626) are the great English compilers of voyages and cosmographies in the sixteenth century.

3. See also the discussions in Margret T. Hodgen *Early Anthropology in the Sixteenth and Seventeenth Centuries* (1964), Charles R. Beazley, *The Dawn of Modern Geography* (1949), and Leonard Olschki *Marco Polo's Precursors* (1943) and "What Columbus Saw On Landing In The West Indies" (1941).

4. "In the Renaissance . . . the ideal age is neither the present nor the future but the past, and a past that is not even Christian: that of the Greeks and Romans. The center is elsewhere, which opens up the possibility of the Other to become, someday, central." (Todorov 1984:109) It should also be noted here that this *use* of Greek Antiquity in sixteenth-century cosmography should not, I think, be confused with the *remembrance* (anamnesis) of Greek Antiquity, which was a decisive moment in the formation of the profounder aspects of the Renaissance and its art and science: "Together with this discovery of the new concept of nature—indeed as part of the discovery itself—the Renaissance experienced an enrichment and deepening of its *historical consciousness*. For now it has new access to the classical Greek world of thought; it has found the way from the Hellenistic philosophy of late antiquity to Platonic idealism. This process is not concerned with making available the genuine Platonic heritage of thought; it is concerned with a real *anamnesis* of Platonic doctrine i.e. with its

renovation in the depths of thought itself" (Cassirer 1963:166). In this sense, the Renaissance was not primarily a reconstruction of classical Greece but more a resurrection of classical Greece.

5. It was, I believe, a movement such as this that Nietzsche had in mind when he wrote, "So much depends upon the development of Greek culture because our entire occidental world has received its initial stimuli from it. An adverse fate decreed that the late and decadent forms of Hellenism should exert the greatest historical force. On their account, earlier Hellenism has always been misjudged. One must know the younger Greece in great detail in order to differentiate it from the older. There are very many possibilities which have not yet been discovered because the Greeks did not discover them. And others have *discovered* the Greeks and later *covered them up again* (Nietzsche 1962:2).

6. His "look" in Sartre's sense. See the discussion regarding "Being-for-Others" and "The Look" in *Being and Nothingness* (Sartre 1953: 340–401).

7. See the discussions in Thomas Kuhn's *The Copernican Revolution* (1957), and also Alexander Koyre's *From the Closed World to the Infinite Universe* (1957).

2. THE OTHER IN THE ENLIGHTENMENT

1. Todorov provides an illuminating formulation of this "problem": "Our chronology has two dimensions, one cyclical, the other linear. If I say, "Wednesday, February 25," I am indicating the day's place within three cycles (week, month, year): but by adding "1981" I submit the cycle to the liniar procedure, since the account of the years follows a succession without repetition, from the negative infinity to the positive infinity. Among the Mayas and Aztecs, on the contrary, the cycle prevails over linearity: there is a succession within the month, the year, or the "cluster" of years; but these latter, rather than being situated in a linear chronology, are repeated exactly from one to the next; . . . one sequence is identical to the next and none is situated in absolute time (whence the difficulties we encounter in translating Indian chronologies into our own") (Todorov 1984:84).

2. Against this one might say, "History in any substantive sense is plural. It is diverse, multiple and particular. . . . Not only are there many histories, there are many chronologies, many *times*, if I may put into accurate plurality here what is usually thought of in terms of single, homogenous flow. It is essentially Western "time" that we have in our minds when we ruminate upon past, present, and future for mankind generally. By a gigantic act of faith we assume that the chronology in which we fit . . . the events and changes . . . of Western Europe is also the Chronology of mankind" (Nisbet 1969:240).

3. This Christian tradition is still, of course, very much alive: "History is conceived as a unity because all historical destinies are under the dominion of a single divine sovereignty" (Niebuhr 1943:107).

4. See also Richard Simon's contemporary *Histoire critique du Vieux Testament* (1678), which first formulated the practice of "criticism" as a method of explaining the meaning of texts, and which maintained that whether it be the *Iliad*, the *Aeneid*, or the *Pentateuch* that is in question, the principles of "criticism" are the same.

5. See also Hazard, "Those beauteous Sibyls that Michelangelo depicted in

the Sistine Chapel were women inspired of God, who, albeit pagans, foretold the coming of Christ, his life, his miracles, his death, and resurrection. The Fathers of the Church made great and fruitful use of the oracles of these prophetesses when converting unbelievers. When, in the books wherein the oracular utterances of the Sibyls are recorded, the Gentiles beheld the mysteries of the Christian faith set down in advance, they were constrained to avow that that faith was divine and true" (Hazard 1954:161).

6. This "anthropological" movement of humanizing the demonic is, I believe, related with Rousseau's deobjectification of "evil" and his profoundly influential socialization of "evil" (against which de Sade would reply with his furious reobjectification and insistence that "evil" is metaphysical and not social). Cassirer marks out the terrain of the problem: with Rousseau's formulation of the original goodness of man, nature, *and* God, "the obscurity of the theodicy problem henceforth seemed completely impenetrable; for if we can neither trace evil back to God nor find its cause in the character of human nature, where are we to find its source and origin? Rousseau's solution of this dilemma lies in his placing responsibility at a point where no one before him had looked for it. He created, as it were, a *new subject of responsibility*, of "imputability." This subject is not individual man, but human society. . . . That is Rousseau's solution of the problem of theodicy—and with it he had indeed placed the problem on completely new ground. He had carried it beyond the realm of metaphysics and placed it in the center of ethics and politics. With this act he gave it a stimulus which continues to work unabated even today. All contemporary social struggles are still moved and driven by this original stimulus. They are rooted in that consciousness of *responsibility* of society which Rousseau was the first to possess and which he implanted in all posterity. . . . Rousseau's solution of the theodicy problem, then, consisted in his removing the burden of responsibility from God and putting it on human society" (Cassirer 1967:75–77).

7. Hazard marks its beginning around 1670. "The worthy, the painstaking, Huet, Bishop of Avaranches . . . undertook the project, in the face of the Egyptian, the Chinese, and other pagan civilizations' preposterously inflated claims to possessing hundreds of thousands of years of existence, of doing nothing less than restoring Moses to his rightful place, namely *first* place. He set out to show that the whole of pagan theology derived from the acts or the writings of Moses; that the gods of the Phoenicians, the Egyptians, the Persians, as well as those of the Thracians, the Germans, the Gauls, the Bretons, and the Romans, all proceeded from Moses. Such was the theme of his *Demonstration evangelica* (1692); and again of his *Quaestiones alnetanae de concordia rationis et fidei* (1690). What, however, he failed to perceive was that his argument was double edged. . . . If there were all those resemblances between the Mosaic beliefs and those of Pagan antiquity, was it Moses who inspired the others, or did those other more ancient races hand on their tradition to Moses?" (Hazard 1954:45).

8. This lies at the heart of the project of the *Encyclopedia* as D'Alembert introduced it in his *Preliminary Discourse to the Encyclopedia of Diderot* (1963): "Probability operates principally in the case of historical facts, and, in general, for all past, present, and future events, which we attribute falsely to a kind of

133

chance because we do not unravel the causes" (1963:18). The concept of causality is what makes the experience of "chance" possible.

9. For those that still persist in maintaining the "obviousness" of causality, i.e., that it is certainty "self-evident" and self-evidently "certain," a passage from Nietzsche: "In every judgement there resides the entire, full, profound belief in subject and attribute, or in cause and effect (that is, as the assertion that every effect is an activity and that every activity presupposes an agent); and this latter belief is only a special case of the former, so there remains as the fundamental belief the belief that there are subjects, that everything that happens is related attributively to some subject. I notice something and seek a reason for it; this means originally: I seek an intention in it, and above all, someone who has intention, a subject, a doer: every event a deed—formerly one saw intention in all events, this is our oldest habit. . . . The question "why?" is always a question after the *final cause*, after the "what for?" We have no "sense for the efficient cause": here Hume was right; habit (but not only that of the individual!) makes us expect that a certain often-observed occurence will follow another: nothing more! That which gives the extraordinary firmness to our belief in causality is not the great habit of seeing one occurance following another but our inability to interpret events otherwise than as events caused by intentions. It is belief in the living and thinking as the only effective force—in will, in intention—it is belief that every event is a deed, that every deed presupposes a doer, it is a belief in the "subject." . . . We have absolutely no experience of a cause; psychologically considered, we derive the entire concept from the subjective conviction that *we* are causes, namely, that the arm moves" (Nietzsche 1970:294–295).

3. THE OTHER IN THE NINETEENTH CENTURY

1. Or, as with Montesquieu's "Persians," with Diderot's Bougainville "savages," the Enlightenment "contrast" assumes, in reversal, the mode of critique of existing, conventional Western morals and customs.

2. See also the discussions in Francis Haber (1959), Charles Gillispie (1959), Loren Eiseley (1958), Christopher Dawson (1960), and Glyn Daniel (1962).

3. James Hutton's brilliant *Theory of the Earth* should also be mentioned here as giving a great impetus to this general intellectual movement while not, however, being directly a part of it, as he appears a "geologist" only through an illusion of the retrospective gaze of an eye already armed with "geology." Hutton was, rather, a "natural historian," of the earth, just as Adam Fergusson was a "natural historian" of civil society: "Hutton has been named a 'geologist' only by our present time. He was, in fact, and regarded himself as a natural historian, doing with the earth exactly what his contemporary Adam Smith was doing with the economic system and what . . . Rousseau was doing with human institutions generally—explaining their development through ongoing and uniform causes" (Nisbet 1969:185).

4. The dangerous threat to orthodox Christianity that chronology and chronometry represented, and the Anti-Christian valorization of time, as it was organized in "geology," was, of course, quite visible to contemporary orthodox Christians: "There is nothing for which cosmogonists ask with more incessant

importunity, than for a great quantity of time. If this requisite be granted they can account for everything; without it they are perfectly helpless" (Macbriar 1843:43). "Geology" was neither the cause nor the result of more secular attitudes; it was a secular attitude.

5. This incredibly pervasive theory of "cultural development," "cultural progress" in anthropology—truth and wisdom are a function of time; and duration itself is an agent of betterment—is almost isomorphic with most models of individual socialization in sociology and psychology. (Indeed, the cultural status and value of childhood will usually reflect, I suspect, the value and status of the "primitive." For example, with Rousseau we don't mature or grow past childhood as much as become alienated from it, and similarly with regard to his "primitive," his "noble savage.") "In sociological writings characterized as normative, the term socialization glosses [rather than explicates] the phenomenon of change from the birth of a child to maturity or old age; . . . the study of these changes as socialization is an expression of the sociologists' common sense position in the world, i.e., as an adult. The notion of socialization [like that of progress] leads to theoretical formulations mirroring the adult view that children are incomplete beings. Investigators have consequently been distracted from the important area of study which is adult-child [European-Other] interaction and the underlying theoretically important problem of intersubjectivity implied in such interaction. Writing about the process of socialization then, has become for me an occasion for exploring the interaction between adults and children [between Europeans and Others]" (Mackay 1973:180).

6. "Unsophisticated and confiding, they are easily led into every vice, and humanity weeps over the ruin thus remorselessly inflicted upon them by their European civilizers. Thrice happy are they who, inhabiting some yet undiscovered island in the midst of the ocean, have never been brought into contaminating contact with the white man" (Melville 1974:21).

CONCLUSION

1. I have myself been guilty of retrospectively using this resource of "culture" in certain sections of this essay wherein I thought I was attempting to uncover and deconstruct certain aspects of Western "culture." Collingwood's teaching that all history is contemporary history, once again, reasserts itself.

2. "If it is incontestable that the prejudice of superiority is an obstacle in the road to knowledge, we must also admit that the prejudice of equality is a still greater one, for it consists in identifying the other purely and simply with one's own "ego ideal" (or with oneself)" (Todorov 1984:165).

BIBLIOGRAPHY

Acosta, Joseph de. 1890 (1590). *Natural and Moral History of the Indies*. E. Grimston, London. Hakluyt Society.

Albritton, Claude C. 1967. *Uniformity and Simplicity: A Symposium on the Principle of the Uniformity of Nature*. New York: Special Geological Society of America.

Arber, Edward, 1885. *The First Three English Books on America (1511–1555)*. Richard Eden, Edinburgh: Turnbull and Spears.

Banier, Antoine. 1740. *The Mythology and Fables of the Ancients Explained from History*. London: A. Millar.

Baudet, Henry. 1965. *Paradise on Earth: Some Thoughts on European Images of Non-European Man*. New Haven: Yale University Press.

Bayle, Pierre. 1965 (1697). *Historical and Critical Dictionary*. New York: Bobbs-Merrill.

Beazley, Charles R. 1949. *The Dawn of Modern Geography*. R. H. Popkin, New York: Peter Smith.

Berger, Peter. 1963. *Invitation to Sociology*. New York: Anchor Books.

Bernheimer, Richard. 1952. *Wild Men in the Middle Ages: A Study in Art, Sentiment, and Demonology*. Cambridge, Harvard University Press.

Bidney, David. 1953. *Theoretical Anthropology*. New York: Schocken.

Black, Max. 1962. *Models and Metaphors*. Ithaca: Cornell University Press.

Blum, Alan. 1974. *Theorizing*. London: Heineman.

Boas, Franz. 1962 (1928). *Anthropology and Modern Life*. New York: Norton.

Boas, George. 1948. *Essays on Primitivism and Related Ideas in the Middle Ages*. Baltimore: Johns Hopkins University Press.

Bock, Kenneth. 1956. *The Acceptance of Histories*. Berkeley: University of California Press.

Bodin, Jean. 1945. *Method for the Easy Comprehension of History*. New York: Norton.

Boemus, Johann. 1555. *The Fardle of Facions, Containing the Ancient Manners, Customs, and Laws of the People Inhabiting the Two Parts of the Earth Called Africa and Asia*. London: John Kingstone and Henry Sutton.

Brehaut, Ernest. 1912. *An Encyclopedist of the Dark Ages: Isidore of Seville*. New York, Columbia University Press.

Levy-Bruhl, Lucien. 1966. *How Natives Think*. New York: Washington Square Press.

Burke, Edmund. 1958 (1756). *A Philosophical Inquiry into the Origin of Our Ideas of the Sublime and Beautiful.* South Bend: University of Notre Dame Press.

Burke, Kenneth. 1937. *Attitudes Toward History.* Boston: Beacon Press.

Bury, Kenneth. 1959. *The Idea of Progress.* New York: Dover.

Cain, A. J. 1954. *Animal Species and their Evolution.* New York: Harper & Row.

Campbell, Donald C. 1961. "The Mutual Methodological Revelance of Anthropology and Psychology," in *Psychological Anthropology.* Francis L. K. Hsu, ed. Illinois: Dorsey Press.

Carr, David. 1974. *Phenomenology and the Problem of History.* Evanston: Northwestern University Press.

Cassidy, Vincent. 1968. *The Sea Around Them, A.D. 1250.* Baton Rouge: Louisiana State University Press.

Cassirer, Ernst. 1953. *Substance and Function.* New York: Dover.

—— 1955. *The Philosophy of the Enlightenment.* Boston: Beacon Press.

—— 1960. *The Logic of the Humanities.* New Haven: Yale University Press.

—— 1950. *The Problem of Knowledge: Philosophy, Science and History Since Hegel.* New Haven: Yale University Press.

—— 1963. *The Individual and the Cosmos in Renaissance Philosophy.* New York: Harper and Row.

—— 1967. *The Question of Jean-Jacques Rousseau.* Bloomington: Indiana University Press.

—— 1970. *The Platonic Renaissance in England.* New York: Gordian Press.

Chiapelli, F., ed. 1976. *First Images of America.* Berkeley: University of California Press.

Collingwood, R. G. 1946. *The Idea of History.* London: Oxford University Press.

Columbus, Christopher. 1930. *Select Documents Illustrating the Four Voyages of Columbus.* London: Hakluyt Society.

—— 1957. *The Four Voyages of Christopher Columbus.* J. Cohen, ed. New York: Penguin.

Comte, August. 1974 (1830–42). *The Positive Philosophy.* Harriet Martineau, tr. New York: A.M.S. Press.

Condorcet, Antoine-Nicholas de. 1950 (1795). *Sketch for a Historical Picture of the Progress of the Human Mind.* J. Barraclough, London: George Weidenfeld and Nicolson.

Conrad, Joseph. 1950 (1890). *Heart of Darkness.* New York: Signet.

Copernicus, Nicolaus. 1947 (1530). *De Revolutionibus Orbium Caelestium,* translated in *Occasional Notes of the Royal Astronomical Society,* vol. 2, no. 10. London.

Créquinière, M. de la. 1705. *The Agreement of the Customs of the East Indians With Those of the Jews, and Other Ancient Peoples.* London.

D'Alembert, Jean Le Rond. 1963 (1751). *Preliminary Discourse to the Encyclopedia of Diderot.* New York. Bobbs-Merrill.

Daniel, Glyn. 1962. *The Idea of Prehistory.* New York: Penquin.

Darnell, Regna, ed. 1974. *Readings in the History of Anthropology.* New York: Harper and Row.

Darwin, Charles. 1962 (1859). *The Origin of the Species and The Descent of Man.* New York: Modern Library.

—— 1903. *More Letters of Charles Darwin.* Seward and F. Darwin, eds. New York:

Dawson, Christopher. 1960. *Progress and Religion*. New York: Doubleday.

Defoe, Daniel. 1961 (1719). *Robinson Crusoe*. New York: Signet.

Degérando, Joseph-Marie. 1969 (1800). *The Observation of Savage Peoples*. Berkeley, University of California Press.

Descartes, Rene. 1961. *Discourse on Method*. New York: Bobbs-Merrill.

Diderot, Denis. 1969 (1772). *Dialogues*. New York: Capricorn.

Dolgin, Janet, David Kemnitzer, and David Schneider, eds. 1977. *Symbolic Anthropology: A Reader in the Study of Symbols and Meaning*. New York: Columbia University Press.

Duerr, Hans Peter. 1978. *Dreamtime, Concerning the Boundary Between Wilderness and Civilization*. New York: Basil Blackwell.

Eiseley, Loren. 1958. *Darwin's Century, Evolution and the Men Who Discovered It*. New York: Doubleday.

Eliade, Mircea. 1959. *Cosmos and History*. New York: Harper and Row.

Elliott, J. H. 1970. *The Old World and the New 1492–1650*. Cambridge: Cambridge University Press.

—— 1972. *The Discovery of America and the Discovery of Man*. London: Oxford University Press.

Evans-Pritchard, E. E. 1962. *Social Anthropology and Other Essays*. New York: Free Press.

Fabian, Johannes. 1983. *Time and The Other, How Anthropology Makes Its Object*. New York: Columbia University Press.

Farb, Peter. 1971. "Doubting Red Indian Stories," *New York Review of Books*, December 16, 1971.

Febvre, Lucien. 1947. *The Problem of Unbelief in the Sixteenth Century: The Religion of Robelais*. 1982. Beatrice Gottlieb, Cambridge: Harvard University Press.

—— 1973. *A New Kind of History*. New York: Harper & Row.

Ferguson, Adam. 1966. *An Essay on the History of Civil Society*. Edinburgh: University of Edinburgh Press.

Feuerbach, Ludwig. 1957 (1840). *The Essence of Christianity*. New York: Harper & Row.

Fontenelle, Bernard Le Bovier de. 1809 (1724). *Conversation on the Plurality of Worlds*. Lackington, tr. London: Allen.

Foucault, Michel. 1965. *Madness and Civilization*. New York: New American Library.

—— 1970. *The Order of Things*. New York: Pantheon.

—— 1972. *The Archaeology of Knowledge*. New York: Pantheon.

—— 1974. *The Birth of the Clinic*. New York: Pantheon.

—— 1977. *Discipline and Punish*. New York: Pantheon.

Freret, Nicholas. 1726. *Réflexions générales sur l'étude de l'ancienne historie*. Paris.

Gadamer, Hans-Georg. 1975. *Truth and Method*. New York: Seabury Press.

Gale, Richard. 1967. "Indexical Signs," in *The Encyclopedia of Philosophy* vol. 4, p. 154. New York: Macmillan.

Garfinkel, Harold. 1970. *Studies in Ethnomethodology*. New York. Prentice Hall.

Gauguin, Paul. 1970 (1890). *Noa, Noa*. New York: Noonday Press.

Gay, Peter. 1966. *The Enlightenment: An Interpretation, The Rise of Modern Paganism*. New York: Vintage.

Gellner, Ernest. 1964. *Thought and Change*. Chicago: University of Chicago Press.

Gerbi, Antonello. 1973. *The Dispute of the New World, the History of a Polemic 1750–1900*. J. Moyle, trs. Pittsburg. University of Pittsburg Press.

Gillispie, Charles. 1959. *Genesis and Geology*. New York: Harper & Row.

Haber, Francis C. 1959. *The Age of the World, Moses to Darwin*. Baltimore: Johns Hopkins University Press.

Hakluyt, Richard. 1965 (1589). *Hakluyt's Voyages*. I. R. Blacker, ed. New York: Viking.

Hale, John. 1967. "A World Elsewhere: Geographical and Mental Horizons," in Dennis Hays *The Age of the Renaissance*. p. 300–350 New York: McGraw-Hill.

Hale, Sir Matthew. 1677. *The Primitive Origination of Mankind Considered and Examined According to the Light of Nature*. London: William Godbid.

Hanke, L. 1970. *Aristotle and the American Indians*. Bloomington: Indiana University Press.

Harris, Marvin. 1966. *The Rise of Anthropological Theory*. New York: Crowell.

Hayden, Hiram, ed. 1961. *The Portable Elizabethan Reader*. New York: Viking.

Hays, Dennis, ed. (1967). *The Age of the Renaissance*. New York: McGraw-Hill.

Hays, Denys. 1966. *Europe: The Emergence of an Idea*. New York: Harper & Row.

Hazard, Paul. 1935. *The European Mind*. New York: Meridian.

—— 1954. *European Thought in the Eighteenth Century*. New York: Penquin.

Helden, Albert Van. 1985. *Measuring the Universe*. Chicago: University of Chicago Press.

Herder, Johann Gottfreid. 1968. *Reflections on the Philosophy of the History of Mankind*. University of Chicago Press.

Herodotus. 1942. *The Persian Wars*. New York: Modern Library.

Herskovits, Melville. 1972. *Cultural Relativism*. New York: Vintage.

Hodgen, Margret T. 1964. *Early Anthropology in the Sixteenth and Seventeenth Century*. Philadelphia: University of Pennsylvania Press.

Horkheimer, Max and T. W. Adorno. 1972. *Dialectic of the Enlightenment*. New York: Seabury Press.

Humboldt, Alexander von. 1848. *Cosmos*. London:

—— 1972 (1811). *Political Essay on the Kingdom of New Spain*. Mary Dunn, ed. New York: Alfred Knopf.

Humboldt, Wilhelm von. 1971. *Linguistic Variability and Intellectual Development*. Philadelphia: University of Pennsylvania Press.

Hume, David. 1956 (1757). *The Natural History of Religion*. H. E. Root, ed. Stanford: Stanford University Press.

Hunter, Richard and Ida Macalpine. 1963. *Three Hundred Years of Psychiatry 1535–1860, A History in Selected Texts*. London: Oxford University Press.

Hutcheson, H. R., ed. and tr. 1944. *Lord Herbert of Cherbury's De Religione Laici*. New Haven, Yale University Press.

Hutton, James. 1972 (1795). *Theory of the Earth*. Germany: Engelmann and Wheldon and Wesley Ltd.

Jordan, Winthrop. 1968. *White Over Black, American Attitudes Toward the Negro, 1550–1812*. New York: Penguin.

Kant, Immanuel. 1929 (1781). *Critique of Pure Reason*. N. N. Smith, tr. New York: St. Martin's Press.

—— 1959 (1791). *Foundations of the Metaphysics of Morals*. New York: Bobbs-Merrill.

140

Karatheodoris, Stephen. 1978. *The Logic and Ethic of Science*. New York: New York University Press.

Kayser, Wolfgang. 1963. *The Grotesque in Art and Literature*. New York: Mc-Graw-Hill.

Koyre, Alexander. 1957. *From the Closed World to the Infinite Universe*. Baltimore: Johns Hopkins University Press.

Kroeber, Alfred. 1966. *An Anthropologist Looks at History*. Berkeley: University of California Press.

Kuhn, Thomas. 1957. *The Copernican Revolution, Planetary Astronomy in the Development of Western Thought*. New York: Vintage.

—— 1970. *The Structure of Scientific Revolutions*. Chicago: University of Chicago Press.

Las Casas, Bartolome De. 1971. *A Selection of His Writings*. G. Sanderlin, ed. and tr. New York: Knopf.

——1971 (1527–1560). *History of the Indies*. New York: Harper and Row.

—— 1975. *In Defence of the Indians*. S. Poole, tr. Northern Illinois University Press.

Lawrence, D. H. 1960. *Studies in Classic American Literature*. New York: Doubleday.

—— 1971. *Movements in European History*. London: Oxford University Press.

Leach, E. R. 1961. *Rethinking Anthropology*. New York: Humanities Press.

Levinas, Emmanuel. 1969. *Totality and Infinity: An Essay on Metaphysics*. Pittsburg: Duquesne University Press.

Locke, John. 1955 (1695). *The Reasonableness of Christianity*. I. T. Ransey, ed. Stanford: Stanford University Press.

—— 1959 (1690). *An Essay Concerning Human Understanding*. New York: Dover.

—— 1969 (1696). *Two Treatises on Government*. New York: Hafner.

Lorant, Stephen. 1946. *The New World: The First Pictures of America Made by John White and Jacques le Moyne*. New York: Duell, Sloan and Pearce.

Lovejoy, Arthur O., Gilbert Chinard, George Boas, and Ronald S. Crane. 1935. *A Documentary History of Primitivism and Related Ideas*. Baltimore: Johns Hopkins University Press.

—— 1936. *The Great Chain of Being*. Cambridge: Harvard University Press.

—— 1960. *Essays in the History of Ideas*. New York: Capricorn.

Lowe, Donald. 1982. *History of Bourgeois Perception*. Chicago: University of Chicago Press.

Lowie, Robert. 1937. *The History of Ethnological Theory*. New York: Rinehart.

Löwith, Karl. 1949. *Meaning in History*. Chicago: University of Chicago Press.

Lubbock, Sir John. 1865. *Prehistoric Times as Illustrated by Ancient Remains, and the Manners and Customs of Modern Savages*. London.

—— 1912. *The Origin of Civilization and the Primitive Condition of Man*. London.

Lyell, Sir Charles. 1863. *The Geological Evidences of the Antiquity of Man*. London: John Murray.

—— 1872. *Principles of Geology; or, On the Modern Changes of the Earth and Its Inhabitants*. New York: D. Appleton.

Macbriar, Robert. 1843. *Geology and Geologists, or Visions of Philosophers in the Nineteenth Century*. London:

MacIntyre, Alisdair. 1967. "Myth," in *The Encyclopedia of Philosophy*, vol. 5. New York: Macmillan.

141

MacKay, Robert. 1974. "Conceptions of Children in Models of Socialization," in Roy Turner, ed., *Ethnomethodology*, pp. 180–193. New York: Penguin.

McHugh, Peter S. et al. 1974. *On the Beginnings of Social Inquiry*. London: Routledge and Kegan Paul.

Male, Emile. 1958. *The Gothic Image*. New York. Harper & Row.

Mandeville, Sir John. 1964. *The Travels of Sir John Mandeville*. New York: Dover.

Manuel, Frank E. 1959. *The Eighteenth Century Confronts the Gods*. Cambridge: Harvard University Press.

—— 1963. *Isaac Newton, Historian*. Cambridge: Harvard University Press.

Marrett, R. R. 1914. *The Threshold of Religion*. London: Methuen.

Mela, Pomponius. 1590. *Di Situ Orbis*. Arthur Golding, tr. London: Thomas Hacket.

Melville, Herman. 1974 (1846). *Typee*. New York: Airmont.

Merleau-Ponty, M. 1962. *Phenomenology of Perception*. London: Routledge and Kegan Paul.

—— 1964. *The Primacy of Perception*. Evanston: Northwestern University Press.

Montague, Ashley, ed. 1968. *The Concept of the Primitive*. New York: Free Press.

Montaigne, Michel Eyguem. 1960 (1588). *The Complete Essays*. New York: Doubleday.

Montesquieu, Chany, de Secondat. 1961 (1721). *The Persian Letters*. J. R. Loy, tr. New York: Meridian.

—— 1966 (1758). *The Spirit of the Laws*. T. Nugent, tr. New York: Hafner.

Morgan, Lewis Henry. 1963 (1877). *Ancient Society*. New York: Meridian.

Morison, Samuel Eliot. 1942. *Admiral of the Ocean Sea: A Life of Christopher Columbus*. Boston: Little.

Niebuhr, Reinhold. 1943. *The Nature and Destiny of Man*. New York: Scribners.

Nietzsche, Friedrich. 1962 (1873). *Philosophy in the Tragic Age of the Greeks*. Chicago: Gateway.

—— 1970 (1888). *The Will to Power*. New York: Vintage.

Nisbet, Robert. 1969. *Social Change and History, Aspects of the Western Theory of Development*. London: Oxford University Press.

O'Gorman, Edmundo. 1961. *The Invention of America*. Bloomington: Indiana University Press.

Olschki, Leonardo. 1941. "What Columbus Saw on Landing in the West Indies," *Proceedings of the American Philosophical Society*, 94, 633–59.

—— 1943. *Marco Polo's Precursors*. Baltimore: Johns Hopkins.

Oviedo, Fernandez de. 1959 (1526). *Natural History of the West Indies*. Sterling A. Stoudemire, tr. Chapel Hill: University of North Carolina Press.

Palmer, Richard. 1969. *Hermeneutics*. Evanston, Ill.: Northwestern University Press.

Parry, J. H. 1961. *The Establishment of European Hegemony 1415–1715*. New York: Harper and Row.

Parry, J. H., ed. 1968. *The European Reconnaissance: Selected Documents*. New York: Harper and Row.

Pearce, Roy Harvey. 1965. *The Savages of America: A Study of the Indian and the Idea of Civilization*. Baltimore: Johns Hopkins University Press.

Penniman, T. K. 1974. *A Hundred Years of Anthropology*. New York. William Morrow.

142

Petty, William. 1927 (1677). *The Petty Papers*. Marquess of Lansdowne, ed. London: Fairfield, N.J.: August M. Kelley.

Philmus, Robert M. 1970. *Into the Unknown, The Evolution of Science Fiction from Francis Godwin to H. G. Wells*. Berkeley: University of California Press.

Playfair, John. 1956. *Illustrations of the Huttonian Theory of the Earth*. New York: Dover.

Pliny. 1956. *Natural History*. H. Rackham, tr. London: Loeb Classical Library.

Popper, Karl. 1968. *Logic of Scientific Discovery*. New York: Harper and Row.

Poulet, Georges. 1956. *Studies in Human Time*. New York: Harper and Row.

Ptolemy. 1932. *The Geography of Ptolemy*. E. L. Stevenson, tr. New York.

Radin, Paul. 1933. *The Method and Theory of Ethnology*. New York: Basic Books.

Ricoeur, Paul. 1965. *History and Truth*. Evanston, Ill.: Northwestern University Press.

Riesman, Paul. 1972. "The Collaboration of Two Men and a Plant." *New York Times Book Review*, October 22, 1972.

Roheim, Geza. 1968. *Psychoanalysis and Anthropology*. New York: International Universities Press.

Rosen, Stanley. 1969. *Nihilism: A Philosophical Essay*. New Haven: Yale University Press.

Rougemont, Denis de. 1966. *The Idea of Europe*. New York: Meridian.

Rousseau, Jean Jacques. 1964 (1762). *Emile*. New York: Baron's Educational Series.

—— 1966 (1762). *The Social Contract: A Discourse on the Arts and Sciences; A Discourse on the Origin of Inequality*. New York: Everyman Library.

Rousseau, Jean Jacques and Johann Gottfried Herder. 1966 (1772). *On the Origin of Language*. New York: Frederick Ungar.

Sagan, Carl. 1975. "The Solar System," *Scientific American*, September 23–27.

Sahagun, B. de. 1932. *A History of Ancient Mexico*. Nashville.

Sartre, Jean Paul. 1953. *Being and Nothingness*. New York: Washington Square Press.

Scrope, George P. 1858. *The Geology and the Extinct Volcanoes of Central Europe*. London:

Slotkin, J. S., ed. 1965. *Readings in Early Anthropology*. Chicago: Aldine.

Solinus. 1587. *Di Mirabilus Mundi*. Arthur Golding, tr. London: Thomas Hacket.

Spinoza, Benedict de. 1965. *Works of Spinoza*. New York: Dover.

Steiner, George. 1971. *In Bluebeard's Castle, Some Notes Toward the Redefinition of Culture*. New Haven: Yale University Press.

Stern, Fritz, ed. 1956. *The Varieties of History, from Voltaire to the Present*. New York: Meridian.

Stocking, George. 1987. *Victorian Anthropology*. New York: The Free Press.

Strabo. 1932. *Geography*. H. L. Jones, tr. New York: Loeb Classical Library.

Swift, Jonathan. 1960 (1726). *Gulliver's Travels*. New York: New American Library.

Taine, Hippolyte. 1965 (1865). *History of English Literature*. New York: Frederick Ungar.

Teggart, Frederick. 1929. *The Idea of Progress*. Berkeley: University of California Press.

143

——— 1960. *Theory and Process of History*. Berkeley: University of California Press.

Tillich, Paul. 1963. *Christianity and the Encounter with World Religions*. New York: Columbia University Press.

Todorov, Tzvetan. 1984. *The Conquest of America, The Question of the Other*. New York: Harper & Row.

Toulmin, Stephen and Jane Goodfield. 1965. *The Discovery of Time*. New York: Harper & Row.

Troeltsch, Ernst. 1958. *Protestantism and Progress*. Boston: Beacon Press.

——— 1971. *The Absoluteness of Christianity and the History of Religions*. Virginia: John Knox Press.

Turbayne, Colin. 1962. *The Myth of Metaphor*. New Haven: Yale University Press.

Turgot, Jean Marie. 1895. *The Life and Writings of Turgot*. London: Longmans, Green.

Turner, Roy, ed. 1974. *Ethnomethodology*. New York: Penguin.

Tylor, E. B. 1865. *Researches into the Early History of Mankind and the Development of Civilization*. London.

——— 1970 (1871). *Primitive Culture*. Gloucester: Peter Smith.

——— 1913 (1881). *Anthropology, an Introduction to the Study of Man and Civilization*. New York: D. Appleton.

——— 1888. "On a method of investigating the development of institutions applied to laws of marriage and descent." *Journal of the Anthropological Institute*. 18:245–72.

Vaihinger, Hans. 1924. *The Philosophy of "As If."* C. K. Ogden, tr. New York.

Voltaire. 1961 (1733). *Philosophical Letters*. E. Dilworth, tr. New York: Bobbs-Merrill.

——— 1971 (1764). *Philosophical Dictionary*. New York: Penguin.

——— 1965 (1766). *The Philosophy of History*. T. Kiernan, tr. New York: Citadel.

Wagner, Roy. 1975. *The Invention of Culture*. Englewood Cliffs: Prentice Hall.

Wallace, Alfred R. 1905. *My Life, A Record of Events and Opinions*. New York: Dodd, Mead.

Wells, H. G. 1961 (1895). *The Time Machine*. New York: Doubleday.

White, Hayden. 1973. "Foucault Decoded: Notes from Underground *History and Theory*. 12(1):24.

White, Leslie. 1949. *The Science of Culture*. New York: Farrar, Strauss & Giroux.

White, T. H. 1954. *The Bestiary, being a Translation from a Latin Bestiary of the Twelfth Century*. New York: Putnam.

Whitehead, Alfred N. 1925. *Science and the Modern World*. New York: Free Press.

Winch, Peter. 1958. *The Idea of a Social Science*. New York: Humanities.

Wittgenstein, Ludwig. 1958 (1953). *Philosophical Investigations*. New York: Macmillan.

Wittkower, Rudolph. 1942. "Marvels of the East: a study in the history of monsters," *Journal of the Warburg and Courtland Institutes*, 5.

144

INDEX

Acosta, J., 8, 11
Alexandre, P., 68
America, discovery/invention of, 30-35
Ancestors: Other as representation of, 94-95; Other as similar to, 68-76
Ancient Greeks, 8; customs of compared with New World, 20-23
Ancients, 8
Anthropology: and the absoluteness of relativity, 119-23; of anthropology, 119; cannot account for itself, 119; Castaneda's challange of, 125-28; construction of with Tylor, 93-100; and evolution, 88-93; and geology, 88-93; interprets everything as culture-bound, 125; man as not yet anthropological, 87; as monologue, 124-27; paradigm revolution of with geology and Darwinian biology, 89-93; similarity with science-fiction, 3-4, 38-39; and Socratic dialogue, 126-27; speaking of rather than speaking to the Other, 127-28
Anthropomorphism, as made possible by causal-mechanical universe, 74-76
Arber, E., 8, 9, 16, 18, 19, 21, 22, 25
Archaeology of anthropology, 1, 2

Aristotle, 126
Astronomy, as critique of Christian cosmology, 35-37
Auerbach, Eric, 129
Aztec, and Roman gods compared, 22

Bachelard, G., ix, 113
Bacon, Francis, 47
Banier, A., 67
Bastian, H. C., 108
Baudet, H., 2
Bayle, Pierre, 55, 56, 69, 74
Beazley, C., 32, 131n3
Bekker, B., 55
Berger, P., 115, 116, 119
Bible: changing status of, 61-64; and establishment of chronology, 58-61; and problem of idolatry, 65-68; prophecy and prediction, 61-64; and scientific prediction, 62-64
Blake, William, 91
Blum, Alan, 1, 5, 116, 126, 131n1
Bock, K., 102
Boemus, J., 8
Borges, J. L., 78
Bosch, H., 13, 45
Boulanger, N., 55
Brant, S., 13
Brehaut, E., 10
Brosses, C., 55, 68

145